tunef

DOUBLE MOUNTAIN BOOKS

Paul H. Carlson, *Series Editor*
Double Mountain Books is dedicated to reintroducing
out-of-print classics of the American West. Primarily
facsimile reproductions, these include recognized works of
continuing value in literature, archeology, history, and
natural history

other double mountain books

tuneful tales

tuneful tales

Bernice Love Wiggins

New introduction by Maceo C. Dailey Jr.
and Ruthe Winegarten

Texas Tech University Press

This book was set in New Century Schoolbook. The paper used in this book meets the minimum requirements of ANSI/NISO z39.48-1992 (R1997).∞

Design by Brendan Liddick

Frontispiece: B. L. Wiggins (left front) and principal William Coleman. Douglas High School, El Paso, Texas. (Coleman is standing directly above B. L. Wiggins on the top step of the building.)

Printed in the United States of America

Library of Congress Cataloging-in-Publication Data
(tk)
Wiggins, Bernice Love, b. 1897.
  Tuneful tales / by Bernice Love Wiggins ; edited by Maceo C. Dailey, Jr. and Ruthe Winegarten.
      p. cm. -- (Double mountain books--classic reissues of the American West)
Includes bibliographical references.
  ISBN 0-89672-485-9 (pbk. : alk. paper)
    1. African Americans--Poetry. 2. Texas--Poetry. I. Dailey, Maceo C. II. Winegarten, Ruthe. III. Title. IV. Series.
  PS3545.I246 T8 2002
  811'.52--dc21
                                        2002003828

02 03 04 05 06 07 06 07 08 09 10 / 9 8 7 6 5 4 3 2 1

Texas Tech University Press
Box 41037
Lubbock, Texas 79409-1037 USA
1-800-832-4042
ttup@ttu.edu
http://www.ttup.ttu.edu

introduction

Bernice Love Wiggins was among the first African-American female poets to be published in Texas. Born in Austin in 1897 but raised in El Paso, Wiggins self-published her first (and perhaps only) book of poetry, *Tuneful Tales*, in El Paso in 1925. She wrote in an era of burgeoning national black literature as writers of the famed Harlem Renaissance and activists of the Universal Negro Improvement Association (led by Jamaican Marcus Garvey) achieved prominence. These new leaders and writers gave voice, passion, and direction to black Americans who sought relief from racism and endeavored to build their communities. Wiggins's poems were written with a similar intent, despite the fact that she was writing from distant Texas.

Though she lived far from any African-American metropolitan area, Wiggins emerged nonetheless in her poems as a brilliant and perceptive poet, capturing the many-sided black experience in El Paso, a remote Texas city perched on the U.S.-Mexico border. She could claim a spiritual and creative kinship with the larger black community through her poetry's illumination of African-American culture and consciousness. Thus her citation as a poet of note by the great Southern black folklorist and critic J. Mason Brewer, who proclaimed Wiggins the female Paul Laurence Dunbar.

Like Paul Laurence Dunbar, Bernice Love Wiggins used standard and dialect English in writing perceptively, sensitively, and humorously about black American life and her community. She focused on local personalities, women's issues, lynchings, African heritage, aesthetics, culture, literary writers, love, political and social growth, the family, the church, and the overall significance of black life in a racialized society of hope, hostility, bigotry, and persecution.

In exploring human motives and activities in the Southwest, Wiggins largely eschewed the folkloric frontier history and emphasis on explorers, adventurers, gunfighters, and military personnel, to write about the ordinary black community or,

to use her words, "wheresoever [her] people chanced to dwell."
Her people were those whose lives unfolded against the back-
drop and legend of the day-to-day Southwest, and by giving us
a glimpse of their world, she is able to herald and laugh with
them as they forged new lives. Wiggins wrote with keen attention to general and nuanced behavior, and managed to breathe
the universalisms of life into poems depicting the lives of
African Americans. In this sense, the tone and style of her
writing are evocative of Dunbar and other great Harlem
Renaissance writers such as Langston Hughes, Zora Neale
Hurston, and Jean Toomer.

Wiggins's poems were published significantly in *The El
Paso Herald*, the *Chicago Defender*, the *Half Center Magazine*,
the *Houston Informer*, and J. Mason Brewer's *Heralding
Dawn: An Anthology of Verse* (1936), but she remained
unknown. There are several reasons for the obscurity of her
book and the limited recognition she received as a poet. She
was self-published; *Tuneful Tales* was her only book-length
publication; El Paso was far from the centers of literary activi-
ty; and she disappeared from the historical record after her
departure from the city in the early or mid 1930s.[1] Her life is
still a great conundrum, though we are able to read her poems.
These poems tell us much about black culture and consciousness in the west and southwest regions where small communities of African Americans resided, and they manifest interrela-
tionships of black life and another side of the flowering of black
writers and artists coming out of the remarkable literary era
known as the Harlem Renaissance.

Wiggins was born on March 4, 1897, in Austin, Texas. Her
early childhood is shrouded in mystery. Her father, J. Austin
Love, was a "laborer, a poet, and a state Sunday School director
for the Holiness Church." According to J. Mason Brewer, the
senior Love was "one of the most outstanding Negro writers of
verse in Texas and the Southwest." One of Love's poems
appeared in a compendium by Josie Briggs Hall of Mexia, the
first known book by a Texas black woman. This is the extent of
current information on J. Austin Love. The origins and life of
Bernice's mother are an even deeper mystery. There is virtual-
ly no extant data on her life. Her background, family, interests,
or childbearing age are all unclear, save that her young child
Bernice is listed in 1902 and 1903 as orphaned at five years of

age. In 1903, Bernice was moved to El Paso, Texas, to live with
her aunt, and subsequently was given the surname of that rel-
ative. As did her father, Bernice Love Wiggins turned to poetry,
and in the first grade was fortunate to have the inimitable
matronly motivator Alice Lydia McGowan as an elementary
school teacher. McGowan eagerly encouraged her young charge
to express herself in rhyme and verse, and Wiggins showed
early promise as a poet.[2]

Enrolled in high school when World War I erupted in
Europe, Wiggins continued her poetry writing at El Paso's
Douglass High School, the lone African-American secondary
educational institution in the city. Douglass High School was
similar to many other black educational institutions in a seg-
regated America. Founded in 1883 to train black students to
the best of their ability, sensitize them to racial matters, devel-
op in them a sense of pride in their people and community, and
spur them to leadership, the school's talented array of teachers
and principals (some of whom had arrived in El Paso from as
far away as Howard University in Washington, D.C.) ensured
that the students would become what scholar W. E. B. Du Bois
called for in his "Talented Tenth" cadre of blacks to uplift the
greater black community. Douglass's principal, William Coleman, a Howard University and Brown University alumnus,
was both a "Talented Tenth" educator and "race man" who
made the El Paso black school a training ground for future
black leadership and responsibility. With alacrity and much
appreciation, Principal Coleman himself was proud to write in
the preface of Wiggins's book, praising her effusively for "poetic
visions born of holy passions, high hopes, and burning enthusiasms." Coleman showed himself to be a wordsmith of uncom-
mon ability in his praise of Wiggins, noting that "the author is
yet young. With the consciousness of a Higher Presence, and
an imagination, divinely enlivened by a light that never was
on sea or land, may she be inspired to sing still more touchingly." Beyond this first publication, however, Wiggins is not
known to have sung poetically "still more touchingly," but
she demonstrated extraordinary talent and promise in this
first book.

There are many interesting questions attending the publication of Wiggins's first book: What was the relationship

between Wiggins and her father? Did he have any impact on
her writing of poems? Did Wiggins, for example, take the
opportunity in 1931 to attend an El Paso poetry reading given
by the famed Harlem Renaissance writer Langston Hughes?
Were Wiggins's poems, as scholar Frieda Werden surmises,
written to be performed similarly to verses of a play or to the
accompaniment of piano music?

Though these questions may remain mysterious, none can
doubt J. Mason Brewer's statement that Wiggins's "deep
knowledge of the psychology of her people is portrayed through
the medium of her dialect verse which at times rises to heights
similar to those attained by the immortal Paul Laurence Dunbar." The El Paso black community in which Wiggins lived
offered much material for this poetic imagination. The black
community expanded from 466 persons in 1900 to 1,330 in
1920 in an overall population increase from 15,140 in 1900 to
37,586 in 1920. Wiggins lived in a progressive and talented
African-American community that had its origins as far back
as Estevanico's appearance in the Southwest in the early 16th
century. African Americans in El Paso, working largely for
either the military or railroad industry in the late nineteenth
century, built a solid community in the second ward in the
southeast section of the city. Churches, schools, businesses, and
professional services were all present in the second ward as
well as prominent organizations ranging from the National
Association for the Advancement of Colored People (founded in
El Paso early in 1910), to the Sunset Lodge Number 76 of Free
and Accepted Masons (Prince Hall affiliate). During the time
that Wiggins resided in El Paso (1903–c.1933), the city also
had its array of exciting and highly motivated African-American personalities. They included Florida J. Wolfe (Lady Flo),
consort to an Irish Lord; Lt. Henry Flipper, the first black
graduate of West Point and later a mining engineer; Zephyr
Chisom Carter, a 1909 alumna of Douglass High School who
went on to Howard University where she became one of the
founding members of the Delta Sigma Theta Sorority; and
Lawrence A. Nixon, a prominent physician who served persons
regardless of race and capacity to pay. It should be noted that
Wiggins published her book at the same time that Dr. Nixon
led the historic struggle to challenge the state's all-white

Democratic primary, taking the suit all the way to the U.S. Supreme Court. Drusilla Tandy Nixon, Lawrence Nixon's wife, organized the black Girl Reserves of the YWCA in El Paso in 1935.

Wiggins also lived in a city with a large Mexican-American community that additionally absorbed Mexican nationals fleeing the Mexican Revolution from 1910 to 1921. El Paso increasing became a terminus for immigrants and foreign workers seeking opportunity and jobs in a city now termed the "Ellis Island of the Southwest." One of the most significant events of this El Paso period was the Tejana laundry workers' strike of 1919, surprisingly supported by a number of the city's white male labor leaders and unions. Race, class, gender, and revolutionary issues were prominent in El Paso, driving poetic and political imaginations about the diversity and direction of the Southwest. In a city becoming increasingly urbanized and shedding its western heritage of cowboy images and occasional shoot-outs in local saloons, Wiggins found an abundance of inspirational topics and wrote accordingly.[3]

Whether using standard, idiom, or dialect language, Wiggins wrote profoundly to find meaning in the black experience, not to demean or denigrate African Americans. We are allowed to see the range of thought, behavior, and interests of African Americans through the many poems of Wiggins. In her poem "The Deacon's Prayer" (p. 29), Wiggins writes:

"Dear Lord, I give myself to thee,
'Tis all that I can do."
Thus humbly prayed the deacon,
and his prayer was never new.

If prayer had a familiar ring and stabilized the would-be saved, religion had its comfort and humor, as in the poem "Religion or Comfort" (p. 59), in which the young poet explains:

Sister Harfield got so happy
She jus' jumped all on my toes,
An' I screamed, dey t'ought I'se happy.
But I wasn't, goodness no's.
Sister Betty Black got bissy,
My dat 'oman sho kin act,

> She jus' hit mos' eve'y body,
> An' I lac' to hit her back.

Christians had demons and moral battles to win in other ways. In "Church Folk" (p. 67), a poem used by J. Mason Brewer to open all of his speeches and featured prominently in his *Heralding Dawn*, Wiggins wrote:

> Folks so bissy watchin' others
> Dat dey ain't got time to pray.
> Goin' 'roun' f'un house to house
> A gossipin' all day.
> I don't talk about no body
> Sister, I ain't got de time
>
> I no's dat I's a Christun, 'cause
> My life is free f'um sin,
> I sho is sick dis mo'nin',
> Is yo' got a little gin?

Wiggins's pronouncements on sensitive political issues reveal both cynicism and optimism, as in "Women's Rights" (p. 56). We cannot dub her a feminist, but perhaps we can characterize her as a "womanist," to use Alice Walker's term. Wiggins exposes resistance to women's rights in her vivid creation of a peevish male persona:

> No, 'oman don't no whut she want
> She change jus' lac' de win'
> An' if she gits to be full boss
> Whut will dis wurld be den?
> I'se sick of all dis talk about,
> De rights whut wimmen want,
> I speck dey'll git 'em do' because
> Hits seldom dat dey don't.

In "The Poetical Farmwife" (p. 55), Wiggins laments the difficulty of composing poetry while doing housework:

> I think about all those sweet nothings
> I read, that the magazines buy,

I know I can write some that's better
And so I sit down just to try.
I hear Billy call from the barnyard,
"Ma! One of them hens got away,"
You can't mix up love lays and chickens,
They don't go together, no, nay.

In "The Man They Couldn't Kill" (p. 42), a small-town rebel becomes a patriot:

We crowned Bill Mason King of Mischief
In our little town.
When ever anything went wrong
We'd know he'd been around
They hung Bill Mason by the neck
High in a tree, one day;
His Ma slipped out and cut him down,
That night he ran away.
But when the country went to war
Bill sailed across the sea,
A soldier, and they say that he
Was brave as he could be.

Folklore and frivolous poetry aside, Wiggins wrote reflectively and meditatively in dealing with human emotions and cerebral moments. Tapping into the theme of black folk rising and borrowing from a statement of noted post-Civil War African-American leader Roscoe C. Simmons, Wiggins intoned in "I Must Share That Rung With You" (p. 40):

Lift thy drooping head, Ethiopia,
Hear us sing now and anon:
"Step up higher, please, my brother,
I want the rung you're standing on."
When by years each rung we've numbered
And there's just one more in view,
Then we'll sing, "Move over brother,
I must share that rung with you."

Wiggins captured the thoughts of those who empathized with the families of the soldiers in "Some One's Son" (p. 96):

> I have no son on the battle field,
> No son in the thick of the fray,
> But for some one's son, O Lord of Hosts,
> On bended knees I pray.

In El Paso of the early 1920s, where the Ku Klux Klan rose briefly to become very powerful in politics and public life, Wiggins focused on the racist organization's known practice of lynchings and asked whether black women should not withhold their sons from serving in war and black men their loyalty until, as she wrote in "Ethiopia Speaks" (p. 38):

> They stop hanging my sons to the branch of a tree,
> Take it back till they cease to burn them alive,
> Take it back till the white man shall cease to deprive
> My sons, yea, my black sons, of rights justly won,
> 'Til tortures are done?

She saluted the poet Paul Laurence Dunbar with these lines in "Dunbar" (p. 100):

> And when at last your lovely soul
> So quietly said goodbye,
> The whole world knew, and knowing
> Heaved a sad and mournful sigh.
> There in your home of rest, sweet rest,
> So very far from here,
> Now when you sing your tender strains,
> The angels all draw near.

In "The Chosen One" (p. 168), Wiggins even celebrates her own choice of a poet's life:

> One offered me gold
> And much luxury:
> One offered me fame,
> A famous man, he.
> One offered adventure
> All offers seem droll!
> So I choose the poet,
> He gave me a soul!

And in the final poem in her volume, she embraces her people in "And Now Goodnight" (174):

I have told you tuneful tales,
Gathered from the hills and vales,
Wheresoever mine own people chanced to dwell.
If the tales have brought you mirth,
Brought more laughter to the earth,
It is well.

The poems in *Tuneful Tales* give full evidence of Wiggins's ability as a poet and a memorable view of black life in the Southwest.[4] Her characters defied the odds to build communities and carve out a palatable semblance of life free from persecution and pain. In the 1980s and 1990s, Wiggins's poems began to receive national recognition in literary biographies and encyclopedias of the black woman's experience.

Ruthe Winegarten was introduced to the works of Bernice Love Wiggins in 1979, when she was working as curator for the Foundation for Women's Resources, sponsor of the exhibition *Texas Women: a Celebration of History*, which toured the state from 1981 to 1982. She and assistant curator Frieda Werden came across Wiggins's work in J. Mason Brewer's anthology *Heralding Dawn*, and found Wiggins's self-published *Tuneful Tales* at the Center for American History. They included some of her work in the exhibit, and Werden's entry for *American Women Writers* (1982) brought national attention to Wiggins. During the 1990s, Dr. Winegarten featured Wiggins's life and work in several volumes about black Texas women. During Black History Month in 1999, when she spoke at the University of Texas at El Paso, we were delighted to learn that we shared an admiration for the work of this great poet. Texas Tech University Press agreed to help us bring Wiggins's work to life again in this new edition, and we anticipate that students, scholars, and lovers of fine poetry will enjoy reading this wonderful collection.

This facsimile edition is made from one of two known copies of the original publication. When I first arrived in El Paso to join the faculty of the University of Texas at El Paso and serve as director of the African American Studies Program, I met

Mrs. Leona Washington, the founder and executive director of
the McCall Neighborhood Center, which is the epicenter of the
cultural and community activities of the city's progressive
African-American population. She casually noted to me a book
in her possession, Bernice Love Wiggin's *Tuneful Tales*, draw-
ing attention to the fine poetry, Wiggins's residency in El Paso
until the 1930s, and the few remaining copies of the book to be
found in the city. Upon taking the book of poems home and
reading it, I was fascinated with the quality of the writing and
sought to research the life of the poet and uncover the fate of
the remaining copies of *Tuneful Tales*. No factual data were
uncovered except that the El Paso Public Library had a copy
and, according to several members of the black community
interviewed, it was believed that copies of the book may have
been destroyed in the late 1950s when the building of Inter-
state Highway 10 cut through a segment of the Second Ward
community and razed the home where the copies of *Tuneful
Tales* had been left. Still, some black El Pasoans have copies of
the book, and McKinley and Bernice Griffin were kind enough
to provide their copy for the reprint.

Maceo C. Dailey Jr.
El Paso, Texas
2002

acknowledgments

We wish to thank the following individuals and organizations for their support and promotion of this republication of the book *Tuneful Tales*. Mrs. Leona F. Washington, teacher and founder and executive of the McCall Neighborhood Center, initiated the project by providing a copy of the book and alerting the authors to the significance of Bernice Love Wiggins's life and poetic career in El Paso. McKinley and Bernice Griffin graciously provided an original copy of the book to be used for the reprint edition. The El Paso Community Foundation, continuing to promote and support the cultural and intellectual life of the city by identifying and encouraging worthwhile projects, assisted generously by providing subvention funds.

Mrs. Ruth Suro-Estrada worked indefatigably to lend us much needed technical assistance, and we thank her for infectious cheerfulness and dedication when faced with deadlines and difficult assignments. Dr. Alwyn Barr, the great historian and scholar of African-American life and culture in Texas, took a particular interest in the life of Bernice Love Wiggins and encouraged and assisted the authors in finding a publisher for the reprint. A note of thanks must also go to Frieda Werden, assistant curator for the touring exhibition *Texas Women, a Celebration of History* (sponsored by the Foundation for Women's Resources), for realizing the importance of Wiggins back in 1981 and including information on the El Paso poet in the exhibit.

Dr. Diana Natalicio, the president of the University of Texas at El Paso, and the history department colleagues of Maceo Crenshaw Dailey are also to be thanked for their support and sharing of resources in ensuring that the history of El Paso and its many different communities will be studied and appreciated within our region, Texas at large, and the nation.

MCD
RW

TUNEFUL TALES

BY

BERNICE LOVE WIGGINS.

1925

EL PASO, TEXAS.

TO

Miss Alice Lydia McGowan
Thanks for your faith in me.
Lovingly,

Bernice.

"Lean down and lift me higher, Josephine.
From the Eternal Hills hast thou not seen
How I do strive for heights? but lacking wings
I cannot grasp at once those better things
To which I in my inmost soul aspire.
Lean down and lift me higher.

"I grope along—not desolate or sad,
For youth and hope and health all keep me glad;
But too bright sunlight, sometimes, makes us blind,
And I do grope for heights I cannot find,
Oh, thou must know my one supreme desire—
Lean down and lift me higher."

Ella Wheeler Wilcox.

INTRODUCTION

The author of these poems was born in Austin, Texas, March 4th, 1897. Through the death of her Mother, January 12, 1902, she became an orphan. At the age of five years, she was taken by her Aunt to El Paso, Texas, where she still lives.

Unfortunately for her, she was not surrounded with a library in the home nor other environments conducive to a refining, cultural, intellectual development that would be an aid to her natural poetic feelings. During her first years in the Douglass School, the high school course of which she finished, she created and recited her own memory verses, the beginning of which she does not remember. She does not know why she preferred this method of expressing herself.

The encouragement of her first grade teacher, Miss A. L. McGowan, influenced her to rely upon herself completely in the creation of original rythmic lines, which became with her, through continued efforts, an easy fixed habit. In her high school course, she learned for the first time something of the art of versification, together with the beauties and suggestiveness of the lines of some of the great English poets.

For several years she has out of her poetic imagination, written many stanzas, some of which she recited and a few were published in the El Paso Herald, Chicago Defender, Houston Informer, and Half Century Magazine.

The poverty, the sorrows, the sufferings, the restricted opportunities of her Race and others lay heavily upon her heart. Unembellished with learned allusions, figures of speech, or other conceits, these poems are the natural breathings of an inspired soul endowed with this highest gift,—"The vision and faculty divine."

These songs are her poetic visions born of holy passions, high hopes, and burning enthusiasms. They are the out-cries of a soul in pain, songs of tenderness; expressions of "hate of wrong;" "agonies of heart and brain."

The author is yet young. With the consciousness of a Higher Presence, and an imagination, divinely enlivened by a light that never was on sea or land, may she be inspired to sing still more touchingly.

Wm. Coleman,
Principal Douglass School.

El Paso, Texas, Dec. 10, 1925.

INDEX

LET US SMILE

———

I could sing a mournful song
With its metre doleful, long,
I could turn reformer, ever shouting "Don't."
I could tell a tale of woe,
Set to measures sad and slow,
      But I won't.

I can sing a cheering lay
Sing of lovers happy, gay,
In a rippling rhyming rhythm that will thrill.
I can make this old world smile,
And forget its cares awhile,
      And I will.

A RACE WITH A CORPSE

I'se had sum awful 'spear'ances
   In my life time, honey, yes;
But when we kept watch wid Jessie
   Dat wus 'bout de wust I gess.
Ain't I nebber tole yo' 'bout it?
   Gess hit slipped my mind sumhow,
'Cause I nebber has fo'got it,
   I kin see it all right now.

T'ings is diff'unt, oh so diff'unt
   Now fum whut dey use to be,
T'ings we used to do, yo'd lafe at
   T'ings yo' do seem queer to me.
Now dis t'ing yo' call "Embalmin"
   Didn't hab dat in my day,
When folks died we washed an' dressed 'em,
   Laid dem out, den laid dem 'way.

Lac' if yo' would die dis mo'nin',
   We would bury yo' nex' day,
But to nite we'd set up wid yo'
   At de chu'ch an' sing an' pray.
Well, we'd fixed up po' Sis Jessie;
   Dressed her in a nice white dress,
An' we had her lookin' better
   Den she eber had, I gess.

In 'dose days I wus right handy
   An' I had a christun heart;
Yo' could always fin' me fo'mos,
   All de time to do my part.
Dey all called me "Prayin' Mary,"
   An' I sho' no'd how to pray;
Pray dem long an' moanful prayers, chile,-
   Beat de preacher any day.

An' dat nite we watched wid Jessie,
　　Chile, I sho' prayed one mo' prayer,
An' dem long an' moanful pleadins'
　　Dat I sont up rent de air.
An' I asked God fo' to hear us,
　　We po' souls of common clay,
An' I begged Him fo' to answer,
　　Dis is part of whut I say:

"Lawd, yo' has heard yo' servant pray
　　In many days gone by,
An' yo' promised dat yo'd always
　　Hear yo' servants cry.
Our sins yo' said yo' would fo'give
　　No matter whut we do,
Yo' said 'What ere yo' ask in faith
　　Dat will I gib yo.'

Lawd, we do no, in days of yore
　　Fo' in yo' book we's read,
Dat yo' did make de blind to see
　　An' yo' did raise de dead.
Lawd, justify our faith in Thee.
　　Lawd, justify our trust!
Move in yo' wondrous way an' give
　　Sis Jessie bac' to us."

I don't no jus' whut happen' nex',
　　But I do no dis much:
Dem moaners cut dey moanin' short
　　An' mos' tore down dat ch'uch.
Fo' I could say 'Amen' an' blink
　　My eyes so I could see,
Dey weren't no body in dat chu'ch
　　But jus' dat corpse an' me.

De corpse wus settin' bolt upright
　　In dat black box, she said:
"Whuts dis, I's in a coffin?
　　Lawd, hab mercy, I ain't dead."

I wus so skaid de laces
  In my shoes jus' popped in two,
An' I all but died when dat corpse cried:
  "Sister Mary, is dat yo'?

Wid dat she started fo' to climb
  Right out dat coffin box.
I wus so skaid I couldn't move;
  My feet done got lac' rocks.
She turn dat coffin over
  An' jus' hit de flo' a sprawl,
Hit chilled my blood right to de bones
  When dat dead 'oman squall.

An' Lawd, de fuss dat coffin made
  When hit fell on de flo',
Wus' nuff to mak' yo' t'ink de day
  Ob Jedgment done cum' sho'.
De corpse wus soon upon her feet
  An' mak'in' straight fo' me,
Den I backs off lac' dis, an' yells:
  "Don't yo' cum close to me."

An' I is hear to tell yo' dat
  Hits sho' sum skairy sight
To see a corpse a walkin',
  Dressed f'um neck to heels in white.
To hear a corpse a talkin'
  Whuts been dead a day or mo',
Ain't funny as yo' t'ink it,
  An' I sho' is one to no.

I spied a open window an'
  I gib my feet a hint,
Dat hit wus time fo' dem to move,
  An' did dey move? dey went!
I hardly teched de window sill,
  Jus' went thru lac' a cat;
You'd thought dat I wus flyin'
  I'd got down so low an' flat.

An' I heard Sis Jessie sayin':
  "Mary, don't run off f'um me,"
But all I said wus dis:—
  "O feet ob mine, jack-rabbits be;
Sweet feet, yo's nebber failed me,
  Yo' done served me well sum how,
An' feet yo' owner begs yo'
  Lawdy, Lawd, don't fail me now."

Did I run? Well run I reckin,
  Me an' my two hund'ed pounds,
Wid de swif'ness ob a rabbit,
  Took dat groun' in leaps an' bounds.
An' dat corpse wus right behind me,—
  Yo'd a thought hit wus a race;
Gess it wus, but let me tell yo',
  I sho' held de winners place.

When I passed de cemetary,
  I shet bofe my eyes right tight,
Den I thought sum' body grab me,
  Chile, dat sho' wus one mo' nite.
I could hear dat corpses feet steps,
  Dey wus gainin' fas' on mine,
A screetch owl scream'd, he said, hit seemed,
  "Hits time to die, hits time."

Den I run thru briers an' thickets,
  An' I jumped a ten foot branch,
Clear'd it to, den scaled a rail fence,
  Whut wus 'round my pappy's ranch.
When I did reach home, dey tell me,
  Dat I mos' tore down de do',
Fo' dat dey could git hit open,
  An' den fell out in de flo'.

Well, dey found Sis Jessie nex' day,
  She wus wand'rin' up an' down,
In de woods, los' weak an' hungry,
  Dressed up in her buryin' gown.

'Twus a trance, she'd had, dey tell me,
　　Dat's a sorter prolong'd sleep,
Hits de nex t'ing to real dyin'
　　An' hits mysteries is deep.

But dat sho' taught me a lesson
　　An' now when I goes to pray,
I don't try to run God's bissness
　　An' I'se keerful whut I say.
I don't go to see no sick folks
　　Or set up wid no mo' dead,
'Cose I no dat hits my duty,
　　But to tell de truf, I'se skaid.

HOME

Well, hit sho' ain't much to look at
    Dats de truf, hit sholy ain't,
Sorter saggin' in de middle
    An' it sho' do need sum paint.
Leaks a little in de kitchen
    When hit sno' or when hit rain
An' dere ain't a winder in it
    Whut ain't got a broken pane.

But I'se happy as a prince could be,
    Beneaf a palace dome,
In dis little shabby cottage
    Dat I'se glad to call my home.
Dats a little word to say it,
    But deres lots whut hit could mean,
De "H" must mean de Happiness
    Wid Hardship in between.

De "O" mus' mean Ole 'Oman,
    'Cause hits her whut mak's home sweet,
She tak's de "M" to mend wid
    An' to mak' good t'ings to eat.
The little "E" means ev'ry'ting
    Dat mak's a home, I gess,
I couldn't start to name dem all
    So I jus' thank an' bless,

The One who measured me my lot,
    An' don't fret 'cause hits small,
When He wus here an' walked on earf,
    He had no home at all.
De birds an' beast all had a place,
    But he jus' had to roam,
Dis shack ain't much to look at
    But I'se thankful cause hits home.

MISS ANNIE'S PLAYING

I has heard a heap ob music
    Played by folks wid lots ob fame,
But I no's one little 'oman,
    Whut could mak' dem players shame.
If yo' 'quainted wid good music,
    Or if yo' is hard to please,
Den yo' oughter hear Miss Annie
    Runnin' up an' down de keys.

When dis little medertation   (1)
    Floats out on hits wings ob love,
Hit seem lak' yo' kin feel yo' soul
    Take wings an' fly above.
An' hit flies right up to heaben
    Light an' gentle on de breeze,
When Miss Annie plays a little chune
    Lak' dis upon de keys.

Maybe den she'll start to strummin'
    On a weddin' march lac' dis,   (2)
Dis ole world gits full ob song birds
    An' yo' heart fill up wid bliss.
Yo' gits hungry fo' a cottage
    An' a little wife to squeeze,
When Miss Annie plays a little chune
    Lak' dis upon de keys.

Den she play dis little lullaby   (3)
    Yo' mammy use to croon,
An' it sets yo' heart to longin'
    When yo' listen to dat chune.
An' yo' wish yo' wus a pappy
    Wid a baby on yo' knees,
When Miss Annie plays a little chune
    Lak' dis upon de keys.

When she no she got yo' feelin'
    Kind ob stupid lak' an' sad,
She jus' play dis little waltz time (4)
    An' hits bound to mak' yo' glad.
Den yo' member how yo' glided off
    In days gone by wid ease,
When Miss Annie plays a little chune
    Lak' dis upon de keys.

An' yo' see yo'sef a youngster (4)
    Prancin' proudly o'er de flo'
Wid a gal dat yo' loved madly
    But her heart wus cold as sno'.
An' she played wid yo's an' tossed it
    Lak' a bag ob ole dried peas,
An' hit hurts yet, when Miss Annie
    Plays dis chune upon de keys.

Yo' kin see de colored sol'jers (5)
    Dressed all up in suits ob brown,
Keepin' step right to de music,
    Proudly trampin' thru de town.
Seem lak' yo' kin hear de bugle
    An' a thrill runs to yo' knees,
When Miss Annie plays a little chune
    Lak' dis upon de keys.

An' to keep dat thrill a goin' (6)
    She plays dis in good rag time,
Yo' kin feel dat thrill a movin',
    Kind ob creepy down yo' spine.
Den so many chills run thru yo'
    Dat if yo'd set still yo'd freeze,
When Miss Annie plays a little chune
    Lak' dis upon de keys.

Hit ain't no use in squirmin' (6)
    'Round an' wigglin' on yo' seat,

'Cose I no' dat ragtime music
　　Acts lak' magic on yo' feet.
But dis little bit ob ragtime
　　Wusn't played fo' yo' to dance,
Spec' yo' 'lig'usus folks would shake yo' feet
　　If yo' had half a chance.

Now don't yo' feel lak' struchin' out　(6)
　　Yo' jints a little bit?
Yo' would too, if yo' wus'nt skaid,
　　Yo' preacher'd hab a fit.
Look at yo' shoulders shakin' dere
　　Lak' leaves upon de trees,
When Miss Annie plays a little chune
　　Lak' dis upon de keys.

Don't dis little bit ob melody　(7)
　　Remind yo' in sum' way
When yo' wus jus' a little scamp
　　An' ev'ry day wus May,
An' yo' had a host ob playmates
　　Fo' to help yo' lafe an' tease,
When Miss Annie plays a little chune
　　Lak' dis upon de keys?

'Member when yo' got religun?　(8)
　　'Way bac' yonder, years ago,
When yo' member how yo' shouted
　　Don't yo' soul git happy do'?
Yo' kin hab a lot ob mem'ries
　　But ain't none as sweet as dese,
As Miss Annie plays a little chune
　　Lak' dis upon de keys.

But yo' bow yo' head in sorrow　(9)
　　When she play dis fun'al dirge
Cause yo' t'ink ob all yo' loved ones
　　Standin' by Ole Jordan's edge,

But sum day yo' gw'ine to jine dem
  So dat sets yo' soul at ease,
When Miss Annie plays a little chune,
  Lak' dis upon de keys.

PIANO ACCOMPANIMENT

1. Meditation   (Flower Song)
2. Wedding March
3. Lullaby   (Sweet and Low)
4. Waltz   (Home Sweet Home)
5. March   (Battle Hymn of the Republic)
6. Ragtime
7. Melody   (Old Black Joe)
8. Hymn or Jubilee Song.
9. Hymn   (Shall We Meet Beyond the River)

KIN FOLKS

I'se always been good natured,
　　An' I'se patient wid out doubt,
But yo' no dat deres a sayin'
　　Dat eben iron wares out.
A sheep is mighty patient too
　　But den I speck hits bad,
To keep on plaguein' at a sheep
　　Until yo' make one mad.

Now my wife's got some kin-folks
　　An' I wants to treat 'em right,
But dey got a way ob comin' down
　　For supper eb'ry night.
Dey ain't nebber been invited,
　　Dey jus' simply 'vites dey self,
But when dey gits thru cleanin' up,
　　Deres neber nuffin' lef'.

Yo' no dere is a sayin'
　　"Dat turn abouts' fair play,"
Deys neber said "Come ober yo'll
　　An' hab a cup ob whey,"
Now mebbe yo' don't b'leive me
　　But hits true as hit can be,
My wife's folks ain't nebber fixed
　　A meal fo' her an' me.

Dey borrows eb'ry t'ing we got,
　　Fum stick-pins up to gold,
I b'leive dey'd borrow if dey could,
　　A piece ob my wife's soul.
But dey is my wife's blood an' kin
　　An' so I don't say much,
Some day I'll lose my temper do'
　　I'se gittin' tiahed ob such.

'Cause heres the thing that riles me mos'
  I'se tellin' yo' a fac',
Dese people borrow t'ings fum us
  An' den don't bring 'em bac'.
But let my wife want sumfin' now,
  An' go to dem fo' hit,
Here's what she git, "I'se sorry,
  But I jus' ain't got a bit."

Now when we git to Heaben soon,
  As we is settled down,
I bet some ob her kin will want
  To borrow ob her crown.
'Cose she'll reach up an' take hit off
  An' to dem sweetly say,—
"Why, Honey, yo' kin hab it,
  I don't need it ennyway."

DEFENDING JOSHUA

I sont Joshua to de sto'
  An' he's been gone a hour or mo'.
Wonder if anyting gone wrong
  Or if dat boys jus' playin' 'long!
Bet he's in sum devilment,—
  Otherwise he ain't content.

Here he cum now, sneakin' in
  Thru de bac,—Josh! Whar yo' been?
Why yo' sneakin' thru de bac?
  Whut yo' got dere in dat sac'?
"Nuffin". Cum here, let me see,
  Boy, whut makes yo' lie to me?

Whar'd yo' git dis Beljum hare?
  "Found it," found dis rabbit, whar?
I wouldn't b'leive dat if yo's dyin',
  Joshua yo' no' yo' lyin,.
I done seed dis hare b'fo'
  An' hit b'longs to ole Sis Flo'.

Done gone off an' stole a rabbit,
  Seem lac' yo' done got de habit.
Stealin', an' den lyin' to,—
  Whut's I gw'ine to do wid yo'?
Keep on 'til yo' caught an' den
  Dey gw'ine a put yo' in de pen.

I'se gwine tell yo' dad, young man,
  Time he's takin' yo' in hand.
I cain't handle yo' no mo',
  But he kin, of dat I sho'.
If he gits his hands on yo',
  He gw'ine beat yo' till yo' blue.

I done fast an' prayed an' cried;
  I done talked, an' begged an' lied,
I'se done all I could fo' yo'
  But don't see no good hit do.
Heres my hair is near 'bout white
  'Cause I worries day an' night.

Wonder why yo' won't behave?
  Yo' is sendin' me to my grave.
Now how cum yo' cain't be good,—
  Ain't I taught yo' dat yo' should?
Joshua yo' sho is bad;
  Don't stan' dere an' grin, I'se mad!

Who's dat cum'in'? I ain't sho'
  But hit walks lac ole Sis Flo.
Yes, dats her, I do declar'
  I smell trubbel in de air:
Hide dat rabbit, Joshua,
  Den git out frum here to play.

Why, good mo'nin', Sister Flo!
  Why yo' puffin' an' blowin' so?
How yo' feelin'? Whut yo' say?
  Whar's Josh? He's out to play.
Stole yo' rabbit? Who, my chile?
  'Oman yo' is talkin' wild.

Yo' has sho' done los' yo' mind,
  Joshua steal? he ain't dat kind.
Now who wus hit tole yo' dat?
  "Buddy Wilson?" Hump! dat brat,
Bet right now he got dat hare
  Hid out in his barn sum whar.

All dat Wilson bunch will steal,
  Buddy's slipp'ry as a eel.
Yo' don't think I'd lie, do you?
  I don't, whut I say is true,

'Cause my grace I wouldn't stake.
  Fo' rabbits, Josh, or my own sake.

Joshua been right here wid me,
  All day an' I no' dat he
Ain't stole nary thing frum yo'.
  Dat's de way yo' people do,—
Overlooks de guilty one
  An' den blames Josh fo' all dats done.

Here yo' nussed Josh when he's small,
  Yo' should be de las' of all
Fo' to try to run him down,
  Yes mam, las' one in dis town.
Say yo' sorry dat yo' came?
  Sorry nuffin, hits a shame.

Makin' lac my boy would steal!
  Yo' don't no how bad I feel,
I ain't mad, but I is hurt,
  Tink how folks will do dey dirt,
Den lay hit on po' Joshua,
  Dats all right, Sis Flo, good day.

Well, she's gone, dat's one mo' lie
  I'll be charged fo' when I die.
But I couldn't let her no'
  Joshua stole her rabbit do',
Why she'd spread hit over town,—
  All de fo' sides, up an' down.

Had to shet her mouf awhile
  Off a Josh,—'cause dats my chile.
'Cose he's bad as he kin be
  But he's mine, he's part ob me.
An' I love him, bad or not,—
  Dats my baby, all I got.

Josh! Cum here, yo' tak dis hare
  Out in to de bac' sum whar.
Kill it, I'm gw'ine mak' a stew,—
  I'm gw'ine add sum dumplins too.
'Cose I'll hab to lie agin
  An' tell yo' dad I kilt a hen.

He eats so fas' he'd nebber no
  Rabbit meat frum fowl, I'se sho',
An' I'll cook it tender, sweet,
  Mak' it taste lac' chicken meat.
But let me tell yo' when hits done
  Don't yo' dare to ask fo' none!

GRANDMOTHER SPEAKS

So that's what you youngsters call dancing,
  This shaking and twisting about,
You tell me that I'm a back number,
  I tell you I'm glad I'm left out.
You twist and you shake and you shiver,
  Yet call yourselves morally clean,
I tell you its low, and its wicked,
  The most vulgar thing I have seen.

And that hollow racket is music,
  You call it a "Jazzy refrain,"
I tell you theres far more harmony
  And music in thunder an' rain.
I'd much rather list when 'tis storming
  To the rough raging roars of the wind,
The night long, than listen an hour,
  To such music, this new "Jazzy' kind.

So thats a ball gown you are wearing,
  And lightly your bosom expose,
Your back is uncovered entirely,
  Don't you feel that you need on more clothes?
You call me old fashioned and fogy,
  But call me whatever you please,
I'll still hold 'tis brazen for women
  To wear dresses up to their knees.

You drink and you smoke and you gamble,
  You tell smutty jokes and you swear,
You have no respect for each other,
  Just strangers to shame and don't care.
It's more than a notion I tell you
  To think what the future will hold,
For its young generations when this one
  Today is so brazen bold.

THE DEACON'S PRAYER

"Dear Lord, I give myself to thee,
    'Tis all that I can do,"
Thus humbly prayed the deacon,
    And his prayer was never new.
For years he'd offered up the same,
    In fact the elders say,
Thus he had prayed when he was young
    And now his hair is gray.

He was a miser truly so,
    The villagers around,
Had marked him as the closest man
    With money, to be found.
For little gave he to his church,
    And less unto the poor,
He loved his Savior in a way,
    But loved his money more.

The deacon's shoes were badly worn
    With that, they did not match.
His coat bore signs of years of wear,
    His trousers bore a patch.
His garb did not belie his words,
    And they that never knew,
Believed, forsooth, to give himself,
    Was all that he could do.

The shepherd who for many years
    Had been the flock's true guide,
At God's command had gone to rest,
    And peace beyond the tide.
And now a man of tender years,
    But truly sent by God,
Had come to tread the selfsame path,
    The late good shepherd trod.

And when the deacon said "Amen,"
  The shepherd new arose,
His glance fell on the deacon,
  But he saw beyond his clothes.
He knew the man before him was
  No victim of distress,
The deacon's prayer was food for thought,
  The Spirit did the rest.

The Spirit gave him utterance,
  He gave his flock the same,
He taught them in a parable:
  "A farmer planted grain,
And when the harvest time had come
  And he had gathered all,
He found no place to store it for
  His barns were far too small.

"The farmer set himself about
  Some larger barns to build,
Said he, 'Soul, we will merry make
  When these, my barns are filled';
But God made answer, 'Fool, oh fool,
  That day will not unfold,
It is my will that you that day
  Make answer for your soul'.

"And so it was; so it will be
  To all that hoard and hold,
The day of happiness and bliss
  To them shall not unfold.
Oh give to God while yet you may,
  My little flock believe,
That he would have you freely give
  As freely you receive.

"Go feed the hungry, help the poor,
  Great your reward will be.

For in the judgment ye shall hear,
  This did you unto me.'
And ye who give yourselves and say,
  'Tis all that I can do,
May hear God say in wrath, 'Depart
  For thee I never knew'.

"And let me in conclusion say
  Prize not the shining gold.
It cannot buy your life from death
  Or save from hell your soul.
It can no more your entrance to
  The Holy City buy,
Than can a camel packed, dear flock
  Pass through a needle's eye."

And at the close of services
  The deacon homeward fled,
When once within his shabby cot
  He knelt beside his bed.
With great tears streaming down his face
  He prayed, "My God, my King,
No more I give myself alone,
  But all I have to bring."

The deacon wears no tatters now,
  As he was wont before,
And he has given more than half
  His gold to help the poor.
The sums he gives to God's own cause
  Are often, and not small,
And when he bows to pray, prays thus,
  "Dear Lord, I give my all."

A LETTER TO SANTA CLAUS

Dear Santa Claus: I'm writing you
   To tell you everything,
That I would like to have you on
   The Christmas Eve to bring.
I do so hope that you can read
   This letter that I write,
My hands are just a trembling
   'Cause its awful tonight.

I'd like so much to have you bring
   A new coat to my Mother,
The one she has is out of style,
   And worn, she needs another.
And, Santy, if its not too much,
   Please have it trimmed with fur,
And then I wish that you would bring
   A nice new dress to her.

Bring her a pair of brand new shoes,
   And please, a velvet hat.
Now that's not all she needs but she'd
   Be very pleased with that.
She never has a thing thats nice
   And new at all, 'cause she
Just does without, and buys for Lu
   And Jack and Bill and me.

My Daddy's always tired when
   His daily work is done,
I know that he'd enjoy an easy chair,—
   Please bring him one;
The kind that has a back that drops
   Just low enough to rest,
All stuffed and leather covered,
   Now I know he'd like that best.

And bring him some tobacco, please,
　'Cause daddy loves to smoke,
He needs some new eye glasses too,
　The ones he had got broke.
So please bring him another pair,
　His poor eyes hurt so bad,
When ere he tries to read that I
　Feel sorry for poor dad.

Lu Baby needs a carriage, please,
　'Cause she can't walk at all,
But she's mighty smart though, Santy,
　For she's learning how to crawl,
But now we have to carry her
　Just every place she goes,
And Lu's a little heavy when
　She has on all her clothes.

Jack wants a little wagon and
　He wants it painted red,
He'd like to have a ball and bat,
　And Billie wants a sled.
And please sir, fill their stockings up
　With everything thats good,
They're going to hang up big ones,
　Oh yes, baby needs a hood.

I'd like to have a new doll please,
　My last one's three years old,
I guess I'd better close now 'cause
　My hands are awful cold.
Now if you can't bring all I ask
　I tell you what you do,
Just leave me out 'cause I won't mind,
　And leave out Baby Lu.

'Cause Baby Lu won't understand
  About the things you bring,
And she'll be just as happy if
  She doesn't get a thing.
As for me; I have my old doll
  And can do without another,
But don't forget the boys and dad,
  And please remember Mother.

NEITHER

I laughed
And my friends laughed with me;
I laughed
But my soul was sad.
I wept!
Thou are sad they whispered,
I wept,
But my soul was glad.

THE CRIPPLE

Drop a coin in my cup my brother,
A coin in my cup, please, I need it.
Behold me a cripple, withered and old,
Bent 'neath the weight of suffering untold,
Drop a coin in my cup, please, I need it.

My age? Why I know when the stars fell, my brother,
I'm eleven and four score, quite aged you see,
And I hope to live on, until I'm a hundred,
Then God will make room in his kingdom for me.

A Christian? Yes, I'm a Christian, brother,
And shall be as long as there's breath in this frame,
I trust the Lord's mercy, and wait for His coming,
And ever adore Him and praise His dear name.

No, I have no children, and I have no kindred,
And no good man ever my burdens did share,
There'll be no one to visit the Field of the Potters,
To seek out my grave and weep over me there.

Yes, I've loved, why not? I was young once my brother,
But he loved not me, I was crippled you see,
Put yourself in his place, ere you blame him, my brother,
Think you could have loved a cripple like me?

Ah, thanks for the coin my brother,
Yes, thanks for the coin, for I need it,
Bent and crippled, and wasted and old,
Tossed on life's billows of hunger and cold,
Ah, thanks for the coin for I need it.

COMMENCEMENT

I stood before an audience vast and grand,
  With trembling lips and eyes with tears made dim,
  A Graduate, and in my frock so prim,
I stood with my diploma in my hand.

The "Graduate's Farewell," each tender strain,
  Rose soft and sweet and fell on listening ears,
  I little thought then that in after years,
Still sacred sweet would be this same refrain.

This truly was the parting of the way,
  Youths greatest play day now would be no more,
  What pained me most and at my bosom tore
The thought that once I longed for this same day.

Commencement! this? Oh how could one pretend
  Were we not leaving much we loved behind,
  Our comrades, friends, our classmates, teachers kind,
Commencement, this? Ah, no, this was the end.

But years have passed since then, long mingled years
  Of love and disappointments, pains and joys,
  Before me stand my own dear girls and boys,
And once again my eyes are dim with tears.

Commencement now for them, their voices blend
  In singing soft and sweet a fond "Farewell,"
  How sad my heart, how sad, I dare not tell,
Commencement now I know means to begin.

Tonight I help to make this audience grand,
  With grateful trembling lips I pray for him,
  My son, a Graduate, so neat and trim,
Stands smiling with diploma in his hand.

Look kindly down on him, Oh Fate, and lend
  Thy hand to guide his ship when rough the sail
  And tho' he falter, may he never fail,
Commencement,—What a distance from the end!!

ETHIOPIA SPEAKS

———

Lynched!
Somewhere in the South, the "Land of the Free,"
To a very strong branch of a dogwood tree.
Lynched! One of my sons,—
When the flag was in danger they answered the call
I gave them black sons, ah! yes, gave them all
When you came to me.

You called them the sons of a downtrodden race,
The Negro you said, in his place must stay,
To be seen in your midst is deemed a disgrace,
I remembered, oh yes, still I gave them that day
Your flag to defend.

And knew when I sent them to your fields of battle,
To suffer, to bleed, to be hewn down like cattle,
Not to them be the plaudit, should victory they win,
History scarcely records it,—too dark was their skin,
'Twas truth I spoke in.

My sons:
How it grieves me for I taught them, 'tis true
That this was their country and for her to die,
Was none less than loyal, the right thing to do,
Brave and loyal they proved and now they ask why
Their country ill treats them, because they are black,
Must I take it back?

Why not take it back?
Until in the South, the "Land of the Free,"
They stop hanging my sons to the branch of a tree,
Take it back till they cease to burn them alive,
Take it back till the white man shall cease to deprive

My sons, yea, my black sons, of rights justly won,
    'Til tortures are done?

Mary wept for her tortured son, in days of yore,
Ethiopia weeps for her sons, tortured more,
Mary forgave, 'twas her Savior son's will,
Ethiopia forgives, but remembers still,
And cries unto God with uplifted hands,
"Innocent bloods bathe the lands."

Lynched!
Somewhere in the South, the "Land of the Free,"
To a very high branch of a very strong tree,
Lynched! One of my sons,—
When the flag drooped so lowly they heeded the call,
I gave them, my black sons, Ah, yes, gave them all,
When you came to me.

I MUST SHARE THAT RUNG WITH YOU

"Step up a little higher, please neigh-
bor; I want the rung you're standing
on."—**Col. Roscoe C. Simmons.**

Let it ring throughout the ages,
　Sing aloud, now and anon;
Step up higher, please my brother,
　I want the rung you're standing on.
Yes, we're climbing, slowly climbing,
　Like the ivy up a wall,
Clinging tightly, glowing brightly,
　Though sometimes a leaf must fall.

Yea, sometimes some force above us,
　'Tempts to push us to the ground,
But we find a niche to cling to
　And on, and upward we are bound.
Often scoffed and much tormented,
　Always called the "Sons of night,"
There's a terrible awakening
　Coming slowly, but with might.

We'll outlive the crimes that taunt us,
　Lynching soon will pass away,
Burning, beating, brutal maiming,
　Shall not long now hold full sway.
We're no shirks, and we're not cowards,
　But out numbered, scores to one,
God made days for every being,
　And each "dog" will claim his own.

In the north, that land of blizzards,
　In the southland, land of light,
In eastern vales, and western deserts,
　You will find us, "sons of night."

Toiling with our fairer brother
    In lowly plane or higher art,
Seldom de we get much credit,
    But we truly do our part.

Whistling, laughing, singing, dancing,
    Jocular and always gay,
In our hearts just one ambition,
    To climb on and win, someday!
O, thank God, that we are climbing,
    We the sons of darkest night,
And we're climbing with a record,
    Full of honor, truth and light.

Lift thy drooping head, Ethiopia,
    Hear us sing now and anon:
"Step up higher, please, my brother,
    I want the rung you're standing on."
When by years each rung we've numbered
    And there's just one more in view,
Then we'll sing, "Move over brother,
    I must share that rung with you."

THE MAN THEY COULDN'T KILL

We crowned Bill Mason King of Mischief
  In our little town.
When ever anything went wrong
  We'd know he'd been around.
He'd burn down people's hay stacks,
  He'd stand and rock the church,
He was the kind the old folks said
  Would never 'mount to much.
He had a gang that followed him,
  Tho' not quite bad as he,
They did just what he told them to
  For he was boss, you see.

Folks said he was a demon with
  Nine lives just like a cat,
He'd been riddled once with buck shot,
  He didn't die from that.
His horses ran away from him,
  And dragged him for a mile,
We found him lying by the road;
  Upon his face a smile.
We thought for sure the boy was dead,
  He didn't blink an eye,
But all at once he laughed and said,
  "Ole Bill ain't gonna die."

Bill saw the picture of a bull fight
  Once and said that he,
Could fight as well as any
  Toreador that there be.
He took his mother's butcher knife,
  His own red flannel shirt,
And only laughed at all the gang
  That warned, "You'll sure get hurt,"

His father's bull was in the field,
   A burly big Holstein,
To me he looked like death itself,
   And he was surely mean.

I won't tell all that happened, it
   Was such a gory sight,
But half the town we lived in
   Went to look at Bill that night.
The bull had tramped him on the ground,
   Then tossed him in the air,
And would have torn him up, I guess
   Had he not landed where
He did, outside instead of in
   The field when he did fall,
And was he dead? Of course not,
   Just disfigured, that was all.

They hung Bill Mason by the neck
   High in a tree, one day;
His Ma slipped out and cut him down,
   That night he ran away.
But when the country went to war
   Bill sailed across the sea,
A soldier, and they say that he
   Was brave as he could be.
One day Bill and his Buddie
   Were sitting side by side,
A shell exploded near them
   And Bill's poor Buddie died.

Bill came home decorated,
   Three countries praised his worth,
The papers told the world he was
   The bravest man on earth.
But one day came a message
   To his Ma, it read this way:

"Bill Mason died of measels,
  We bury him today."
They say that fate is fickle,
  It surely was with Bill,
Just think, he died of measels,
  The man they couldn't kill.

A HOME FOR MOTHER

I'se jus' received a letter
  Frum dat baby boy ob mine.
He's doin' well, he tells me
  An' his fam'lys' doin' fine.
He's beggin' me to leave dis house
  An' cum an' lib wid him;
He t'inks hit would be better
  'Cause my eyesight's gittin' dim.

He says dat hit ain't safe fo' me
  In dis ole house alone.
Dere's no one to po'tect me
  Since de chilluns dad is gone.
Yes, gone to res' an' dats jus' why
  I holds dis place so dear,
De memories ob all I's loved
  An' los' is all right here.

Frum de attic to de bas'ment,
  All dese rooms dey secrets hol',
An' I hate to leave de ole home
  Even do' I'se gettin' ole.
Why no place on earf could mak' me
  Feel lac' dis place does, I no,
An' I wouldn't be contented,
  So hits wrong fo' me to go.

De reward ob years ob labor
  All around here smile at me
An' I t'ink ob how we struggled
  Frum de day dat we wus free,—
Me an' Dad, to be sumbody
  An' to mak' our chillun fine;
Well, we did it, thanks to heaven,
  Schooled dem all, an' dere wus nine!

An' we bofe worked hard an' faithful
　　So's to raise our chillun right;
An' prayed to God to guide dem
　　An' po'tect dem wid his might.
An' now all ob dem is married
　　An' dey all is doin' well,
An' I'm happy, proud an' thankful,
　　Mo' den I hab words to tell.

All ob dem hab room fo' "Mother,"
　　An' dey all say, "Cum to me,"
But yo' see Jim, he's de baby,
　　An' he kinder feels dat he
Should cum first befo' de others,
　　But de res' don't feel dat way,
So to hurt nobody's feelins
　　Right on here I'm gw'ine to stay.

Why hits not de least bit lonesum,
　　Daddy's spirit's always here;
I kin feel hit an' den sumtimes
　　In de twilight I kin hear
Him a callin' softly to me,
　　An' I answers, "Here I is,"
Den I feel sum arms aroun' me
　　An' I no dat dey is his.

I am thankful to de chillun
　　An' I'm glad dey love me so,
An' I no dey'd mak me welcome
　　But I jus' don't want to go.
Why dey daddy wouldn't lac' hit,
　　If I'd go so fur away,
Frum de home we made together,
　　So right here I'se gw'ine to stay.

Stay right here till God de Father,
　　Calls me to dat home ob Love,

Den I no I'll be contented,
  In another home above.
For dere'll den be no mo' changin',
  Settled fo' eternity,
An' de chillun whut's now scattered,
  Kin cum home to Dad an' me!

THE LAST LESSON

The class had met to say farewell,
   Commencement time was near,
Bright smiles belied a saddened heart,
   A 'kerchief hid a tear.
Long had we known that we must part,
   But oh, how very sad each heart!

The Master of the class arose,
   "Ah, time has flown so fast,"
Said he, "This lesson that I teach
   Today shall be the last,
We've spent such happy hours here,
   The parting makes me sad and drear.

"Have I been too exact?" said he,
   "Or seemingly unkind?
Perhaps, but bear this with you
   Throughout this life you'll find,
That where like methods are employed
   The best results will be enjoyed.

"I pray that down the span of time
   Success shall crown each name,
I would that none would falter, fail,
   Nor play a losing game.
Ambitious ever be and try,
   To live a life that cannot die.

"With conscience clear, I dare to say
   That I have done my best
I have not wholly failed, but what
   Will be the future test?
For like the parable of the seed,
   I've sown in bad soil, rocks, 'mid weeds.

"The greater part of these seed sown
  Did fall in fertile soil,
God grant, the coming years to bring
  Rich harvest for my toil.
Then you like farmers plant again
  And reproduce the precious grain.

"Now if you have a parting word
  For me, arise and speak,"
He added, while a tiny tear
  Stole gently down his cheek.
Each student arose to have his say,
  Common sentiment ran this way:

"Professor, we can never pay
  The much we owe to you,
You've done your duty and if we
  Have to ourselves been true,
If we have learned each lesson taught,
  We count all fears of failure naught.

"We love you just for what you are,
  Not what you might have been,
You have been stern, perhaps, but kind,
  You are a man of men.
And may the future for you hold
  Health, wealth, and happiness untold."

"I thank you for each word of praise,
  'Tis flowers rare you gave,
And they are mine to cherish
  While I dwell this side the grave.
We cannot hear the nice things said
  About us after we are dead.

"Now let us sing, 'Blest be the tie
  That binds," each tender strain

Rang like the bells at eventide,
  As each voice joined refrain
A sacred sadness held full sway,
  When came the words, "Now let us pray."

The Master bowed his worthy head,
  In sad and tender voice
He offered up a prayer that made
  Each soul that heard rejoice.
God bless the man and grant that we
  Prove all that he would have us be.

THE PREACHER AND THE BEAR

We'd been holdin' a revival
    In a Brazos Bottom town,
If I'd call de name yo'd no
    Jus' where its at.
An' de preacher whut we had
    Wus called de Reverend Doctor Slown
As fo' preachin'—Whew! he sholy
    Could do dat.

He had preached fo' us fo' three weeks,
    Den de folks twelve miles away,
In a little town called Cheapside,
    Sent fo' him to cum one day.
An' dey wrote, "Put on yo' armour,
    Satan's Army's in dis land,
An' deys mos' nigh conquered Brother,
    We, yo' Master's little band."

Well, one evenin' jus' at sun down,
    Brother Slown paid us a call,
An' he said, apologizin',
    "Gess I'll have to bother yo'll,
But I wants to use yo' lantun;
    Dese here nights is dark, yo' no,
An' I'se got to walk to Cheapside,
    An' de bes' way I kin go

Is right thru de Brazos Cane brake
    Den down thru de big ravine."
"Man," I says, "dem bears will git yo',
    Biggest bears yo' ever seen
Lives down in dat Brazos Cane brake,
    Yo' don't want no lantun light,
Whut yo' wants is broadest daytime,"
    But he tell me, "Dats alright,

Fo' de Lord will fight my battles
   In Cane brake, or anywheres,
An' wid him beside me, Brother,
   I need hab no fear of bears."

Well, we give him our lantun
   An' I offered him my gun,
But he simply wouldn't take it,
   Said he'd hab no use fo' one,
'Cause thru faith alone he'd conquer,
   So I said, "I gess yo' right,
But dem bears is gw'ine to git you,
   'Cause hits mighty dark tonight."

Thru de cane brake went de preacher,
   An' his little lantun light,
Lighted up de path befo' him
   An' his song rang thru de night:
   "I no my Lord is a man ob war!
   I no my Lord is a man ob war!
   I no my Lord is a man ob war!
      Fo' he fought my battles
      Long time ago."

He wus deep down in de cane brake
   When he hears a rustlin' soun'
An' yo' no 'twus only natshul
   Dat de man would look aroun',
An dere stood a bear, a big one,
   My dat preacher wus so scared,
Dat his hair whut had been nappy,
   Fairly straightened on his haid.
An he prayed, "O Lord, I need yo'
   Won't yo' please to cum on down,"
While he prayed de bear wid one paw,
   Knocked de preacher to de groun'.

An' he hit de groun' a rollin',
   But almos' befo' he fell,

He wus up, once mo' de bear struck
  Den de preacher wid a yell,
Took an' hurled his little lantun
  Right in to de big bear's face,
Den his feet took wings, I tell yo',
  Bear an' preacher had a race.

When he made hit to my gallery,
  He wus mos' nigh scared to death,
"Man," I says, "Good lan', whuts had yo'?"
  "Bears," he whispers, out ob breath.
Dat po' man was nearly naked,
  He wus scratched an' bruised an' tore,
I felt sorry but I never
  Lafed so hard, I gess befo'.

Well, I washed his wounds an' dress 'em,
  Den I put him in de bed,
An' when he had got all settled,
  Jus' to tease him sum, I said:
"Tol' yo' dat dem bears would git yo',
  Hits a wonder yo' ain't dead,
Thought de Lord's fought all yo' battles?"
  Den de preacher grinned an' said:
"Well, de Lord's all right fo' sumthings,
  Fo' revivals an' fo' sech,
But fo' fightin' bears do' brother,—
  Gess he mustn't like dat much."

FROM KENTUCKY

His hair was as white as the cotton that blows
    In the fields of the fair sunny South,
His eyes bore the gleam and the twinkle of youth,
    And a merry smile played on his mouth.
His skin was the color of baked "yellow yams,"
    It was red, it was black, it was brown,
Fair nature had mixed the three colors on trial
    And much pleased had handed them down.

"How old are you uncle?" I asked the old man,
    "Wal, honestly chile, I don't no',
I'se been in dis ole wurld for many a day,
    An' I 'spec' I'se eighty er mo'."
"Well where were you born? Have you always lived
        here?"
    His chest he threw out like a turkey,
With pride in his voice and with smiles in his eyes,
    He replied, "I wus born in Kintucky."

"Well, shake, so was I," and I gave him a coin,
    Five dollars it was, in bright gold,
Then I bade him godspeed, and hastened away.
    I next day to a friend of mine told
Of the whiteheaded old man from the State of my birth,
    His reply, "That was Old Jim the Lucky,
He's been round here every day of his life,
    He's never been near Old Kentucky."

THE POETICAL FARMWIFE

I think about all those sweet nothings
  I read, that the magazines buy,
I know I can write some that's better
  And so I sit down just to try.
I hear Billy call from the barnyard,
  "Ma! One of them hens got away,"
You can't mix up love lays and chickens,
  They don't go together, no, nay.

I've wandered away down the hillside,
  Carrying my book and my pen,
And there I would write just like lightning,
  To get all the pretty thoughts in.
The thoughts get all mixed up with turnips
  That Bill wants for dinner today,
You can't mix the cook pots and poetry,
  They don't go together, no, nay.

One day Billy came from the dairy,
  I said with my prettiest smile,
"Now, Billy dear, please don't disturb me,
  I really must write for a while." .
"Come skim this milk, Janey," he blustered,
  "I've got to go help with the hay,"
You can't mix the sonnets with churning,
  They don't go together, no, nay.

WOMEN'S RIGHTS

I jus' don't 'prove ob wimmen
   Runnin' 'round fum place to place,
A talkin' 'bout dey want dey rights.
   Hits jus' a plum disgrace,
Dey mos' all got mo' rights right now
   Den dey can carry straight;
Hits awful how de wimmen folks
   Is carrin' on ob late.
Deys tryin' to pile mo' on dey bac's
   Den whut deys gw'ine to tote
Ain't dey got 'nough 'sponsebilities!!
   How cum dey wan'na vote?

T'ree thousand years now, mo' or less,
   De men's been doin' fine,
A runnin' all de politicks,
   An' t'ings along dat line.
Dey'd better let 'em keep hit up
   Lord nos hits fo' de bes',
When wimmen starts to runnin' t'ings,
   Dey mos'tly starts a mess.
Take Adam fo' example,—he
   Wus doin' fin' alon'
Den up steps him a 'oman
   An' he was made to moan.

I reckin' I'se ol' fashin, but
   Deres mo' den me will say
A 'oman's place is in de home,
   An' dere she ought to stay.
In dis wurld dere mus' be chillun,—
   If de wimmen lac' de men,
Gw'ine hang erround de ballot box,
   Who's gw'ine to raise 'em den?

Hit jus' simply wasn't 'tended,
  Take de beasties ob de wood,
De she beast min' de younguns an'
  De he beast bring de food.

Dey say dat wimmens gw'ine to rule
  Dis entire wurld sum'day,
I truly hope dat time won't cum,
  'Till I'se been laid away.
No, 'oman don't no whut she want
  She change jus' lac' de win'
An' if she gits to be full boss
  Whut will dis wurld be den?
I'se sick ob all dis talk about,
  De rights whut wimmen want,
I speck dey'll git 'em do' because
  Hits seldom dat dey don't.

WORRIED

Night's a gettin' stormy,—
  Ain't dat norf win' wild!
Whar on earf is Lancy?
  Wonder whar's my chile.
Gess he had a 'gagement
  He couldn't 'ford to miss,
Oughter be at home do
  On a night lac' dis.

Hush, somebody hollered!
  Wonder whut's de row;
Wish my Lanc' would cum home,—
  Whar's he any how?
'Spec sumbody'll brain him
  Sum dark lonely night;
Dere's been lots ob killin's
  Whut ain't cum to light.

Hear dat dog a howlin?
  'Fead to shet my eyes;
If dey'ed bring Lanc' feet first
  'Twon't be on surprize.
Dere I'se talkin' random
  But hit mak's me cry,
'Cose if I'd lose Lancy,
  B'leive my soul I'd die.

Did I hear a whistle?
  Yes suh! Dat's dat boy,
An' dat whistle sho' do
  Fill my heart wid joy.—
Cum on to de fi'yah,
  Yo's a purty sight,
Good fo' nuthin' rascal,
  Whyn't yo' stay all night?

RELIGION OR COMFORT.

Whar is dem ole slides ob mine;
Won't yo' please to be so kind
As to fin' dem fo' me Vee?
Dese here shoes is killin' me!
Nebber in my life befo'
Has my po' feet ached me so.
Why dey feel jus' lac' hot coals,
Done been plastered to de soles;
All de bones whuts in 'dem ache,
Seem as if dey gw'ine a break.
I'se a wreck, dis heart ob mine
Gone to makin' double time.
Dere's pains all ober me,
I'se one chunk ob misery.

Hush! don't talk to me right now;
Whut yo' talkin' 'bout anyhow?
Why'd I buy my shoes to small?
Dese shoes ain't too small a tall.
Didn't I habe dem fitted? Sho,
Gess de sto' man ought to no',
Don't t'ink 'cause yo' feet is big
Mine is; I don't hab to rig
Mine in gun boats, lac' yo', see?
Futhermo' don't talk to me.

How wus meetin'? I don't no'
How it wus,—I jined chu'ch do'
Shouted right in to de fol'
Yes, dey got me on de rol'.
But I ain't got no 'ligun Vee,
I jined so dey'd let me be.
I'd been on dat moaners bench
A week, an' hadn't budged a inch,
Dis, yo' no' wus closin' night,

Dey caps wus set fo' me alright,
So dey moaned an' prayed an' sing,
But I jus' ain't heard a t'ing,
'Cause dese feet hurt me so bad,
Dat dey mos' nigh drove me mad.

So I jus' rocked to an' fro
Lac' dis, dey said, de Spirit sho
Wus workin', an' I mus'n't grieve
Him any longer, 'cause he'd leave,
An' Elder Rambeau; po' ole goose,
Said "Yo' might at well turn loose,
Fo' we means to see yo' thru,
We'll stay right here all nite wid yo'."
Gess yo' no how dat sound Vee
Wid my feet jus' killin' me?
Well, dey fairly had me dizzy,
Den de devil he got bissy.
"Whyn't yo' jine yo' fool," said he.
"Den dese folks will let yo' be."
So I jines; de whole chu'ch shouted,
I did to, so no one doubted,
Dat I'd made it thru alright,
Chile, dey had sum time tonite.

Sister Hartfield got so happy,
She jus' jumped all on my toes,
An' I screamed, dey t'ought I'se happy,
But I wusn't, goodness no's.
Sister Betty Black got bissy,
My dat 'oman sho kin act,
She jus' hit mos' eve'y body,
An' I lac' to hit her bac'.
Ole man John Jones got to runnin'
An' a jumpin' up an' down
'Til I almos' lafed, 'cause honest
Dat man looked jus' lac' a clown.
Hattie Dodge jus' snatched her wig off

An' den th'owed it in de air,
Her heads slick as any door nob.
She ain't got a lick ob hair,

Sister Morris jumped de benches,
Sister Whitehead fairly danced.
Elder Rambeau got so joyful,
He jus' clapped his hands an' pranced.
Brother Louden la'fed an hollered,
Sister Lizzie Neal jus' cried,
But if yo' had seen her face do',
Vee I no yo' would a died.
Sister Lu Green drapped her baby,
An' her ole man tried to die,
But dat sho' is one tough youngun,
Why it didn't eben cry.
Brother Fulmer chews terbacker,
His ole mouf stays wet wid juice,
An' he kissed me, I'd a hit him
But den, Vee, whut wus de use?

So I played my part mos' proper,
I would shout an' jump a while.
An' den 'tend lac' I wus cryin,
So dey couldn't see me smile.
Lawd, dey sho' wus glad to git me,
Dey'd been after me fo' years.
All de ole folks sed "God bless yo',"
An' dey face wus wet wid tears.
It wus awful to deceive dem,
But I had to do it, Vee.
Why I couldn't git no 'lig'un
Wid my feet jus' killin' me.
An' dere ain't no use to worry,
Hit's done happen, 'cose I'se sorry.

I is scheuled fo' baptism,
Sunday mo'nin' but I isn't

Gwine to tak' no chance to drown
Sunday I'll be out ob town.

Take dem shoes an' hide dem, Vee
Sum place where I'll nebber see
Dem no' mo' I'se near 'bout dead
An' I'se gwine straight to bed.

HAS YO' SEED HIM?

So yo' wants to sleep here stranger?
  Wants to sleep here fo' de night?
Well I reckin' yo' is weary
  'Cause yo' sho'ly looks a sight.
Cum, I always done fo' others,
  Whut fo' me I'd hab dem do,
An' I'se got a boy, too, stranger,
  'Way frum home tonight lac' yo'.

Folks hab cum frum Filadelfy
  An' deys cum here frum New Yo'k;
I'se seed folks frum all dem places
  Ob whut Jacob use to talk.
When I ask dem has dey seed him
  Dey say "No'um, he wus'nt dere,"
None ob dem ain't seed my Jacob,
  Dey ain't seed him anywhere.

Has yo' seed him? Seed my Jacob?
  Has yo' seed him anywhere?
He's got eyes whuts bright an' sparklin'
  Black an' curly is his hair.
Yes suh, dats his picture stranger,
  An' he always wo' dat smile,
Always sweet an' good wus Jacob,
  Nebber wus a hateful chile.

If yo' see him, tell him stranger
  Dat his mammy say "Cum home,"
'Cause his daddy's gone to glory
  An' I'se ole an' all alone.
Tell him dat I wants my baby,
  Tell him I'se mos' grieved to deaf,
Tell him dat I'se cried about him
  'Til dere ain't no mo' tears lef'.

All his t'ings I keep in order
  Lac' I dun befo' he lef;
I don't let nobody tech dem
  Hates to tech his t'ings myself.
I keep water in his basin,
  An' fresh flowers on de stan',
When he do cum bac' my Jacob,
  He'll fin' t'ings all spick an' span.

I keep all his baby trinkets
  Locked up safe in dis ole chest,
Wait a min'et an' I'll sho' yo',—
  Dis cap use to be his bes'.
An' he wo' hit jus' on Sundays
  When I took him out to church,
Yes suh, an' dat boy outgrowed hit
  'Fo he got to wear hit much.

Now yo' wouldn't t'ink my Jacob
  Eber wo' dis little dress;
Hits de fust one whut I made him,
  Does I love hit? Goodness yes.
Made hit all upon my fingers
  Ev'ry stitch a stitch ob love,
An' I knitted him dese stockin's
  Why dey fit jus' lac' a glove.

He wo' dese when he wus crawlin',
  See here where his toes cum thru.
'Cose I no dat all dis stranger
  Don't mean nuffin much to yo'.
But dese shoes all wo' an' ragged
  Mak's me feel a little sad,
'Cause dere ain't no tellin', stranger,
  Jacobs shoes now might be bad.

An' he's libal to be hungry
  An' his health hit might be po'.
An' who no's he might be beggin'
  Lac' a tramp frum do' to do'.

But I hardly think so, Jacob
  Wus as proud as he could be,
An' he'd die fo' he go beggin'
  'Cause he's jus' dat much like me.

Funny t'ing how boys when ramblin'
  Never stop to think ob home,
Never stop to write dey mammy's
  Whut sets worryin' while dey roam.
Seem lac' dey gits trabblin' fever
  An' keeps trabblin' far away;
Well, I pray God fo' to let me
  Live to see my boy sum day.

'Do his baby days is ober
  He's a baby still to me,
Jus' de same as when he uster
  Croon his chune upon my knee.
An' sometimes here in de stillness
  Seems lac' I kin hear his feet,
Goin' pit-pat, dis house ober
  Mak'in' music soft an' sweet.

Yo' smile lac' my Jacob, stranger,
  An' I lac' to see yo' smile.
Whut yo' sayin? Don't I no yo'!
  Lo'd hab mercy, heres my chile.
An' to t'ink I didn't no him,—
  Baby, Honey, whar yo' been?
But hit wouldn't mak' no diffunce
  If yo' been off in de pen.

Cum on bac' into de kitchen,
  Let me fix yo' sumpun eat,
Let me pull dem shoes off ob yo',
  So dat yo' kin res' yo' feet.
Hush! don't tell me not to do it
  I no whut I want to do

Set still here 'til I unlace dem,
    Jacob I'm so glad hits yo'.

Dere now honey, deres yo' slippers,
    Now I'se goin' to fix yo' bed,
So yo' eat a bite, den lay down,
    Mammy specks yo' nearly dead.
Son, I sho' is glad to see yo',
    No'd yo'd cum bac' home sumday,
No'd yo'd cum bac' to yo' mammy,
    Jacob is yo' goin' to stay?

Whut yo' say? Yo' cum to git me
    Goin' to take me home wid yo'?
Look here, boy, is yo' done married?
    Don't I lac' hit? 'cose I do.
Put yo' arms around me honey,
    An' jus' hold yo mammy tight;
Ise been waitin', waitin' for yo',
    An' I sho' is proud tonight.

CHURCH FOLKS

Good mo'nin' Sister Anderson;
  How yo' cum on t'day?
Yo' ain't cumplainin? Well dats good,
  I wish I felt dat way,
But I ain't much,—I'se all stov' up,
  It's mos'ly in my knee,
I'se mighty 'fraid dat rumatiz
  Is cumin' bac' on me.
You wusn't out to meetin' Sunday,
  Yo' say yo' couldn't go?
Well, dats too bad, but den I 'low
  Yo' didn't miss much do.

I'se t'inkin' whut a shame it 'tis
  De way de chu'ch folks do.
Tain't many good ole christuns
  In de chu'ch lac' me an' yo'.
De chu'ch jus' full ob hipercrits,
  Jus' 'tendin' lac' dey's good
Dey aint got no mo' lig'un
  Den whut's in dis piece ob wood.
De preacher, he's so properish,
  Dat I don't lac' him much—
But dats de kind of man de hi'tones
  Want's in our chu'ch.

Deres a mighty little li'gun goin'
  'Round now whuts wurf while,
Seem lac' all de good ole christuns
  Done laid down dey grace fo' style.
Yo' can se'ch de conju'gation
  Fum de pulpit to de bac',
An' won't fin' enuff pure li'gun
  Fo' to stop de smallest crac'.

Deres a heap ob so called christuns
  What jus' libs a life ob shame,
Why de sinners an' de chu'ch folks now
  Is migthy nigh de same.

Deres Deacon Green,—he's got a voice
  Lac' tom cats on a fence,
An' you wish dat he'd quit singin'
  Fum de min'it he commence.
He cums to chu'ch, wid all his airs,
  Jus' mos' nigh dressed to dea'f.
He oughter keep his mou'f shet,
  'Count ob licker on his breaf.
An' when dey calls on him to pray
  He mak's his prayer so long
To keep f'um drappin' off to sleep
  I'se 'blige to hum a song.

Dey got ole Annie Johnson
  Up dere singin' in de choir.
Now she cain't sing, an' no' she cain't,
  Den whut is her desire
Fo' bein' up dere wid de res'?
  De reason's plain to me,—
She wears fin' clothes an' dere she sets
  So all de folks kin see,
Tryin' to 'tend lac' she so young,
  Dat 'omans ole as sin
I 'spec' when I's a baby,
  She wus takin' comp'ny den.

Dere's ole Mis' Sildy's daughter,
  Jus' las' month she jined de chu'ch,
An' las' week she give a break down ball
  Yo' eber hear of sech?
I no' dat hits her bisness,
  But bac' dere in our day
Our Ma an' Pa'd a kilt us
  Had we carried on dat way.

Hit's a shame befo' de Master
   How folks lets dey younguns do,
'Tain't many mudders raisin' up
   Day crops lac' me an' yo'.

Ant Mari wus out las' Sunday,
   Now dat ole soul jus' ain't right
Wearin' all dat store bought glory
   On her head, ain't she a sight?
Had·it puffed all out an' twisted
   Right in style to, bless yo' soul,
Fixed up lac' a gal of sixteen,
   Hits a shame, 'cause she's too ole.
Ain't no sense fo' folks whuts her age
   Over styles to rage an' rave,
One foot in, de other ready,
   Fo' to slip right in de grave.

Yo' oughter seed ol gran'pa Elec!
   My, dat ole man sho is spry,
Ain't it awful? Why dat ole soul's
   Mighty nigh too ole to die.
Talkin' 'bout he's gwine a marry
   Soon as he kin fin' a wife.
How dese ole folks cut sich capers
   I cain't see to save my life.
'Cose he's grown, an' got a right
   To do jus' as he please,
'Tain't my bisness, but he oughter
   Spen' mo' time upon his knees.

Folks so bissy watchin' others
   Dat dey ain't got time to pray.
Goin' 'roun' f'un house to house
   A gossipin' all day.
I don't talk about no body,
   Sister, I ain't got de time.

Keeps de cross right on my shoulder
  An' I hews right to de line.
I don't cast my lot wid sinners
  An' I lives above all sin,
'Cose I takes a little toddy,
  Fo' my health's sake, now an' den.

I jus' don't b'lieve in talkin' 'bout
  De way dat people do,
Dis little 'scussion whut we had
  Is jus' 'tween me an yo'.
But, chile, de chu'ch folks jus' ain't right
  Mos' ob 'em los' dey grace
An' dere's a mighty heap ob dem
  Won't see de Master's face.
I no's dat I's a Christun, 'cause
  My life is free f'um sin,
I sho is sick dis mo'nin',
  Is yo' got a little gin?

THE MISSUS GLIMM AND ME

The Missus Glimm across the way
    Is always neat and clean,
Jim says she's jus' the tid'est thing
    That he's mos' ever seen.
Why she keeps ev'rything in place
    An' primps herself each day,
Jim wants to know how cum' it is
    That I cain't be that way.
I'd like to be jus' like Mis' Glimm,
    As neat as neat can be,
But she ain't got a whole houseful
    To take care of like me.

Mis' Glimm ain't got nobody but
    Herself an' ol' man Glimm,
I've got six healthy girls an' boys,
    A cat, two dogs an' Jim.
A dandy flock of handsome fowls,
    A cacklin' in th' yard,
A cow to milk, a house to clean,—
    An' housework pretty hard.
I cain't be neat like Missus Glimm,
    I don't have time to be,
For she ain't got a hundred things
    To do each day like me.

Mis' Glimm prepares her evenin' meal
    An' then prepares herself,
Then sets an' waits for ol' man Glimm,
    I don't have primp time lef'
In fac' my Jim cums home sum'time
    Before' his supper's done
An' he gits cross tho, even then,
    He finds me on the run.

Hot tears with prespiration mix,
    I yearn for sympathy,
An' Jim starts railin' 'bout Mis' Glimm—
    Well, she don't work like me.

She does not have to lay a patch
    When little frocks git torn,
Nor does she even have to wash
    Wee faces ev'ry morn.
She never has the task I have
    When shadows gather deep,
Of tellin' bed time stories an'
    To lull wee folks to sleep.
Nor does her dress, all nice an' starched,
    Git mussed frum neck to knee,
Frum holdin' laughin' girls an' boys,
    Upon her lap like me.

Jus' when it pleases her Mis' Glimm,
    Sets down to take her rest,
When I set down it's mos' to hol'
    A baby to my breast.
But when those chubby little hands
    Within my bosom steal,
I can't help but wonder jus'
    How poor Mis' Glimm would feel
To be a baby's mother, an'
    Who knows it may be she
Sets in her cushioned easy chair,
    An' envys humble me.

Mis' Glimm on Sunday goes to church
    An' carries ol' man Glimm,
I fix my healthy bunch of six
    An' send them too, with Jim.
I stan' and watch them out of sight
    An' think that how for years,

I've 'tended to their ev'ry want
    An' soothed their tiny fears.
I wish that I could work for them
    Through out Eternity,
I pity poor Mis' Glimm, 'cause she
    Ain't got a flock like me.

Jim choose me for the mother of
    His children, an' that he
Might have his wish, I walked with Death,
    Six painful times, you see.
I've given him a wife's true love,
    An' them a mother's care,
Jim choose me for his helpmate an'
    I try to do my share.
No, I'm not neat as Missus Glimm,
    I don't have time to be,
But I'm a mother for Jim's six,
    An' they are proud of me.

THE SCOLDING

Cum on 'way frum dat tela'fone,
Dats all yo' does de whole day long,
Whut yo' talkin' 'bout ain't no count
An' hit don't cum to no amount.
Here, don't yo give me no bac' talk,
I'll beat yo' so tell yo' cain't walk.

Say, whut's I gwine to do wid yo',
Why yo' jes' t'inks yo' grown, yo' do!
Now eber since yo' got eighteen
Why yo' jes' t'inks yo'se'f a queen,
Yo' may be grown, but I is to,
I bet I'll knock sum sense in yo'.

Young lady, listen to de truf,
As long as yo' is neaf my roof,
Yo' gwine to mind me on de dot,
Whether yo' wants to min' or not.
I slaves all day lak' sum ole fool,
Jus' so dat yo' kin go to school.

An den yo' up and shows yo'se'f,
Lak yo' de onl'est 'oman lef.
Now dats whut I git, dats my pay,
Dats my thanks, yo' sassy ole jay.
Here I jus' wears de same ole dress,
Neighbors all pokin' fun, I gess.

Spends mos' nigh all I mak' on yo',
Indeed I does, yo' no I do.
Jus' so dat yo' kin look refine,
Does all I kin to mak' yo' shine.
Now yo' gwine fine me wrong sum day
An' deys gwine hab to lay yo' 'way.

Here I aint had a hat fo' yares,
My Sunday's dress am full ob snares,
Look at dese shoes, how bad deys worn,
Sum times I wish yo' wusn't born,
'Cause I lives lak' a tramp, I do,
A tryin' to tak keer ob yo'.

Stop mumblin', whut wus dat yo' said?
Yo' say yo' wish dat yo' wus dead?
Dat shows jus' how much sense yo' got
'Cause yo'll be dead now lak' as not
'Fo yo' is ready,—wish yose dead!
I gess dese boys done turned yo' head.

'Cause eber since yo' got a beau,
Yo' been a actin' queer, I no.
Why now yo' nebber sings a song,
Yo' use to sing de whole day long,
An' sum how yo' don't seem so gay,
Now whuts de trubble anyway?

Has yo' done fell out wid yo' Jim?
Um huh, so dats it, so its him.
My gracious honey, don't cry now,
Why yo' don't want Ole Jim no how,
Say he's goin' wid yo' cousin Lou?
Why she ain't haf as good as yo'.

If dat ain't jes' a plum disgrace,
Ole Lula flountin' in yo' face,
But cryin' mak's yo' face look ole,
So don't yo' cry, yo' jes' be bol',
We'll sho' ole Lu a t'ing or two,
I tell yo Honey whut yo' do.

Yo' dress yo'se'f an' go to town,
An' buy a pretty party gown,
An' on tomorrer at dat ball,

Why yo' will look de bes' ob all,
Den Ole Jim he'll cum bac' to yo',
Sho'; dats de way I use to do.

So run on Honey, git dat dress,
An' git de swellest, git de bes',
I'm gwine to let dese people see
Dat dey shan't hurt whut b'longs to me,
An' loves a funny t'ing, I no,
I wus a gal once, long ago.

MAMMY'S PRIDE

Whut yo' askin' me fo' sonny?
  Has I saw yo' cane an' hat?
No, I ain't,—say is I bissy?
  'Cose; how cum yo' ask me dat?
Standin' right dere lookin' at me
  Wid my han's all in dis do'
If yo' want me fo' to help yo'
  Fin' yo' t'ings, why jus' say so.

If dis bread ain't whut hit should be
  Den hits yo' whut bares de blame,
If hits soggy, sad an' heavy,—
  Yo' gwine eat hit jus' de same.
Got to have sumbody help yo'
  Fin' yo' t'ings lak' you'se a child.
Whyn't yo' member whar yo put 'em?
  Boy, yo' mos' nigh drives me wild.

Sumetimes I jus' stop an' wonder
  How cum yo' don't lose yo' head,
Spec' yo' wud, if hit wud cum off,—
  Dere's yo' cane dere on de bed.
Yo' don't nebber look fo' nuffin',
  T'ink dats all I got to do
Is to stop, when I is bissy
  An' jus' fly an' wait on yo'?

Here's yo' hat, yo' helpless baby,
  Now whut else yo' want me do?
Is yo' tie straight? Wait a minit,
  Dere's a spec' o' dirt on yo'.
Hol' still here an' let me bresh it
  Offen yo' befo' yo' go,
I don't want yo' lookin' wusser
  Den sum step chile or hobo.

Boys ain't nuffin much but trubble,
  Yo' de wust I ebber seen,—
Got a hank'cher in yo' pocket?
  Let me see if hit is clean.
Um huh,—an' now whut yo' huntin'?
  Dem yo' gloves right ober dere,
Let's see if yo' shoes is shinin',
  Hold still, let me bresh yo' hair.

Dere now, kiss me, yo' ole "Buggah,"
  I jus' loves yo' thru an' thru,
Yo's as helpless as a baby
  But yo' mammy's proud ob yo'.
Wonder if yo'll miss yo' mammy
  When yo' tak' yo'self a wife,
Ain't no 'oman gw'ine to spile yo'
  Lak I has all yo' life.

An' hit sholy will be lonesum
  'Round dis house when yo' is gone,
Don't no whut on earf I'll feel lac'
  Wid no baby to wait on.
Why my life will jus' be empty,
  An' I won't no whut to do,
Bless yo' heart, yo' mammy fusses,
  But she loves to wait on yo'.

WHAT IS LOVE?

I asked a brown eyed maid, she dropped her head,
"I cannot tell, yet I'm Love's slave," she said.

I asked the pansies growing in the dell,
"We love," said they, "and yet we cannot tell."

I asked the wild geese as they southward flew,
They only flapped their wings, they never knew.

I asked a mountain, standing firm and proud,
"Ah me, I know not," still he kissed a cloud!

I asked the wild wave as they kissed the shore,
"Tis something strange," they sighed, with gentle roar.

I asked the winds that blow where none have trod,
"If thou wouldst know," said they, "go ask thy God."

And straightway to the Father I did go,
"My child," said he, "in heaven thou shalt know."

FRIENDS AND FLOWERS

Fresh for a day,
   Tomorrow they shall be
Faded and dead,
   Dear friend, this gift from thee!

And like the flowers,
   Soon you too shall be
Far, far away,
   Dear friend, so far from me!

Shall I forget
   The flowerets so dear,
Or the friend that gave them,
   My heart to cheer?

Not so, dear one,
   For after years have flown,
Memory shall bide me
   Claim both mine own.

TO TARRY HERE

I watched a lonely funeral train,
  Wend slowly on its way.
I bowed my head, some weary soul
  Has found eternal day.
Death; how I shudder at the thought
  And what is there to fear!
There's rest, and peace beyond the grave,
  Why should I tarry here?

Here in this place of sighs and song,
  Where things just come and go,
And every mite of joy we share,
  Is doubled thrice with woe.
And mine has been a weary lot,
  Still, as the time draws near,
I have no great desire to leave,
  I want to tarry here!

CONSCIENCE

"'Tis wrong," my conscience said to me,
"Oh fie, how great the pleasures be,
'Tis life and love therein for me,
'Tis not so wrong," quoth I.

"Beware," said she, "the painted lie
Such pleasures only gratify
A space, they do not satisfy."
I heeded not the plea.

I heeded not the worthy plea,
Now I'm as wretched as can be,
For conscience has forsaken me,
Yea, conscience grieved did flee.

WHY NOT?

I sought to prove a friend in deed,
And helped a brother, sore in need,
When he I lifted from the mire,
To place me there was his desire.

An outcast, wanderer of the street,
Once more I placed upon her feet,
And then I paid in grief and shame,
She robbed me of my once good name.

And so, in anger, loud I swore,
To help the fallen one no more,
Then said my Lord, "Behold thou me;
Betrayed, denied, I died for thee!"

THE TAILOR'S SONG

Plying a needle from morn until night,
  Mending a hole or darning a tear,
Ripping a seam that somehow wasn't right,
  Placing a button first here and then there.
Things to remodel that once were thought perfect,
  Sadly I sigh as I rip out the seam,
Just like the garment I too, must be defect,
  Just so has fate ripped and shattered my dreams.

Often I sing as my needle I ply,
  Hear ye my song and believe all is well
While my heart aches and my eyes àre not dry,
  Nobody cares, so there's no one to tell.
No one to tell that, my heart is nigh breaking,
  The world wants a song and none of my woe,
Tears softly fall on the garments I'm making,
  Tears softly fall, but I sing as I sew.

Sing as I sew, but Oh, me, I'm so weary,
  Weary of sorrow and longing and pain,
Each passing hour grows dreary, more dreary,
  Oh! will I ever be happy again?
Nay, for out there neath the sod and the starlight,
  Sleeps my own darling, my heart and I know
That until Death comes, with me all is dark night,
  And tears shall fall, though I sing as I sew.

HALLOWE'EN

Day cain't come fo' me too soon,
  See dat queer speck cross de moon,
Nuthin' don't appear jes' right,
  Dis, yo' no is witches night.
Yes, tonight de witches ride,
  Wid de devil side an' side.

Long befo' de break ob day,
  Spirits leave dey graves, sum say,
How dey sway an' skip an' prance,
  An' de devil jines de dance.
Win' hit mak' de music sad,
  While de spirits dance lac' mad.

SNOW

Dey tell me dat a poet's got
A beauty lovin' soul,
An' sees sumt'in' pretty in mos' anyt'ing,
When other folks is grumblin' 'bout
De weather hot or cold,
He jus' chunes up his heart an' mak's it sing.

I'se t'ink'in' 'bout de poet whut
Sung praises to de sno'.
Sum how I jus cain't figger he wus right.
I don't see how a body could
Fergit hits cold, I's sho',
An' pertend dey loves sno' jus' 'cause hits white.

My eyes is runnin' water an'
My throat is awful so',
My bac' aches an' my feet been bit by frost,
I'se 'feared I got newmonyah,
'Cause my jints is achin' so
My sides is full ob mis'ry an' I'se cross.

I'se 'feared I got newmonyah,
An' still I'se nearly froze.
Out doors de sno' is two or three feet deep.
I dar'sant go to bed at night,
I jus' set up an' doze,
De bed hits jus' so cold dat I cain't sleep.

I reckin' dat ole poet whut
Sung praises to de sno'
Nebber waded out in hit to earn his bread,
Nebber had icicles hangin' in
His whiskers, 'cause I'se sho'
He'd abused dem little fleecy flakes instead.

PECANS

"I wish I had some peekuns"
Our Mary said, said she,
"If I just had some peekuns
  I'd be happy as could be."

"Is dey flowers?" ask Aunt Maggie,
  "If dey is, dey new to me."
"Oh my no, why they're nuts Aunty
  And they grow upon a tree."

"Well I'se nebber heard ob dat name,
  How yo' spell it?" Aunty said:
"P-e-c-a-n-s, Peekuns,"
  Mary spelled, and tossed her head.

"My how t'ings do change," said Aunty,
  "Go on chile an hab yo' way,
But dese things yo' callin' peekuns,
  Was 'bucons' bac' in my day."

DANDY JIM

Ise awaitin' yo' returnin',
    Dandy Jim.
My po' heart's mos' sick wid yearnin'
    Dandy Jim.
Is yo' always gwine to roam,
Ain't yo' nebber comin' home,
Don't yo' no I'se all alone,
    Dandy Jim?

I'se ask ev'ry body 'bout yo'
    Dandy Jim.
Life jus' ain't wurf while wid out yo'
    Dandy Jim.
Dandy, since yo' went away,
Life to me don't seem so gay,
How long is yo' gwine to stay,
    Dandy Jim?

All de song birds seem to warble
    "Dandy Jim,"
An' de medder brook jus' gurgle
    "Dandy Jim"
An' de gentle sighin' breez,
As hit whisper thru de trees
Seems to murmur words lac' dese:
    "Dandy Jim."

I'se a prayin' God to hold yo'
    Dandy Jim,
In His arms may He enfold yo'
    Dandy Jim.
An' if He has willed it so,
Dat yo' don't come bac' no mo',
In sweet res' we'll meet, I'se sho',
    Dandy Jim.

SAMMY JOE

Folks say I mak' a diff'runce wid de chillun'
Sammy Joe's de one dey say I loves de bes'
  But I don't, I loves dem all
  Jus' a lac', de big an' small,
Sammy Joe, he jus' acts diff'un f'um de res'.

He's de one whuts always beggin' "please" to help me,
Wid whut eber dat I do f'um day to day,
  He'll be hangin' 'round de house
  Jus' es quiet es a mouse
When de other chilluns off sum' wheres at play.

When I'se been away f'um home sum'days a workin'
An' cum's draggin' in, as tiahed es I kin be,
  Do' de res' ain't 'round no where,
  Sammy Joe will sho' be dere,
Standin' at de gate a waitin, jus' fo' me.

He'll throw his arms around me an' he'll kiss me,
Den he'll say to me, "Yo' tiahed to deaf I no
  But I'll be a man sum' day
  An' dat day ain't fur away
Den I'se nebber gwine to let yo' work no mo'."

His voice is lac' de brook down by de medder
Hit jus' gurgles, full ob music, kinder sad,
  He's jus' one big chunk ob love
  An' de Angels up above
I'se af'aid is kinder jealous ob de lad.

Jus' six months fo' Joe wus born, his daddy lef us,
Went away to live an' res' wid God above,
   Joe's de image ob his dad,
   Got his ways, too, bless de lad,
Jus' so gentle, jus' so kind, so full ob love.

Folks say I mak's a diff'unce wid de chillun,
But I don't, for airry one ob dem I'd die,
   But hits jus' lac' dis, yo' see
   Sammy Joe brought bac' to me,
Part ob whut de Lawd took f'um me, gess dats why.

MARKET MEAT

We buys our meat f'um butcher shops,
　Since we moved in to town.
Today I bought sum sausage,
　'Twus de bes', dey sed, dats groun';
But when my Mandy cooked it up
　I took one tiny bite,
I couldn't swaller dat, becaus'
　It didn't taste jus' right.

My mem'ry went a skippin' to
　De farm; bac' in dem days
We lived a simple country life
　Wid simple country ways.
I thought about hog killin' time,—
　The oldest boys an' me
Got up fo' day to start our job,
　Got up 'bout ha'f pas' t'ree.

We'd mak' a rippin' roarin' fire,
　Tote water f'um de spring,
An' fill de kittles fo' to scald
　Our hog, an' we would sing.
Sing loud, because dat mo'nin' breeze
　Whut fanned de flames to sparks,
Jus' fanned our souls to music sweet
　An' we jus' sang lac' larks.

We'd kill an' scald an' scrap our hog,
　An' by de time de sun
Had started peepin' o'er de hills
　Our wurk wus mos' nigh done.
Side meats, an' liver; hams an' ribs,
　Lights, leaf and sausage meat,
When we made sausage in dem days,
　'Twus sausage fit to eat.

No sweepin's an' no offal, but
 Jus' rich, sweet tender loin,
We'd pack it down in crocks of lard,
 To keep, an' hit kept fine.
We had spareribs wid dumplins,—humph!
 An' when we'd cook de head
We'd bile a pot ob collards
 An' bake cracklin's in de bread.

We's done moved f'um de country now
 An' has to buy our meat,
But hit jus' tak's my appetite,
 'Cause hit ain't fit to eat.
We nebber miss de joys we has
 Until deys passed away;
I sho' do miss de country,
 An' I'se gw'ine bac' sum day.

HARD TIMES

Gettin' mighty dark out do's,
  I spec' it gw'ine to sno',
Ev'ry lump ob coal is out
  An' I cain't buy no mo'.
Money's awful skase wid me,
Hard times is at de do',
Sho' do seem lak' God done turn
  His bac' upon de po'.

Gess I better hobble out
  An' pick up ev'ry bone,
Bones mak's mighty splendid fire
  When all de coal is gone.
Spec' I has de 'grippe dis year
  Or hab newmonyah sho',
Sho' do seem lak' God done turn
  His bac' upon de po'.

Sum one stole my fedder bed
  I sunned out on de gras',
An' my kivers is so wo'
  I'se 'fead dat dey won't las'.
Seen sum hard times in my days,
  But none lak dese befo',
Sho' do seem lak' God done turn,
  His bac' upon de po'.

Use to set up ev'ry night
  As late as I desire,
Goes to bed right wid de hens,
  Now, cain't affo'd de fire.
If ole Crimp don't hurry by
  I'll freeze to deaf I no,
Sho' do seem lak' God done turn
  His bac' upon de po'.

SIGHS OF A SOLDIER

I'se here to do my duty, an' I trys, but I'll be bound,
  If dat biggity ole Sarjunt don't quit bossin me around,
Sum day I'se gw'ine crazy, I'se jus' gw'ine to lose
      my head,
  An' dey's gw'ine to fin' dat Sarjunt wid his carcus
      full ob lead.
Dere's a heap ob boys aroun' here whuts as lazy as kin be
  But he don't nebber bother dem, jus' always picks
      on me.

One day I'se in de baff house, scrubbin' down my
      dirty skin,
  I hears dis sawed off Sarjunt blat "Is Private Amos
      in?"
"He's in de baff house," sum one said, "He just brung
      in de mail,"
  An' to de baff house here he struts, wid "Repo'te fo'
      detail,"
"Say man, go git sum body else, I'se bissy as kin be
  An' I'se tired too, I jus' got in, how cum yo' pick
      on me?"

He 'lows, "Whose givin' orders here?" Alright, I sez,
      I'se cumin'."
  "Why surtainly, I no yo' is, mak' 'ace, an' cum a
      runin'!"
"Man, whyn't yo' let me 'lone, I sez, yo' tole me whut
      to do?"
  Sez he, "Don't hand no two fo' ones, I'll send yo'
      to de 'Lu'."
I sho' do wish he had, I'd been as happy as could be
  Fo' in de guard house its a cinch, he couldn't pick
      on me.

He's made me do mos' ev'ryt'ing, he's eben had de gall
 To make me shine lak' silver, all de nail heads on
  de wall,
An' he has made me pick up eve'y match stick layin'
  'round,
 He's made me pick tobacker up dat he'd spit on
  de ground,
He swore he didn't do it, but 'twus plain as hit could be,
 Ole Sarjunt did dat dirty trick, so he could pick on me.

When I has served my time out, an' dey tell me I kin go,
 Why if I live three thousands years, I won't cum bac'
  no mo',
Dey say dat yo' ain't loyal to de flag if yo' don't fight
 An save her frum her enemies; de fightin' parts
  alright,
I'se willin' 'nouf to fight fo' her, an' die too, if need be,
 But I'll nebber give another Sarjunt chance to pick
  on me.

I aint got no religun, so I'll miss dat land on high,
 I don't keer much, I tell yo', 'cause I got a reason why,
Dere ain't no place in Heaben fo' a man lak' Sarjunt
  Green,
 He'd mak' de angels lose dey grace, dats honest, he's
  so mean.
If I don't git a chance on earf, I'll follow where he be,
 An' mak' him drink hot lead, fo' eve'y time he picked
  on me.

SOME ONE'S SON

I have no son on the battle field,
  No son in the thick of the fray,
But for some one's son, O Lord of Hosts,
  On bended knees I pray.

Some dear little mother, worn and gray,
  Has given her only son,
The son she cherished, hoping some day,
  To have him to lean upon.

Some true little wife, a sister sad,
  And somewhere a sweet heart trim,
Tonight while the stars watch over the world,
  Bows down and prays for him.

No son have I on the battle field,
  No one in the thick of the fray,
Dear Lord of Hosts, sincerely I kneel
  For some one's son I pray.

LINES

So dark the way, O Lord of Light
    I am afraid.
Afraid that I might lose my way,
Afraid, dear Lord, that I might stray,
Stray from the path that leads to day,
So dark the way, O Lord of Light,
    I am afraid.

SOMEWHERE

———

Somewhere the sun is ever shining,
Somewhere the heart knows naught of pining,
Somewhere the task is done
Somewhere the victory won,
        Somewhere.

Somewhere the soul has none of sorrow,
Somewhere we think not of tomorrow,
Somewhere we will find
Rest for body, and for mind,
        Somewhere.

BUSTER

A little head of golden curls,
Two eyes more gray than blue,
A little body free from pain
Sleeps 'neath the sod and dew.

Two feet that made such music rare
As o'er the house they trod,
Are pillowed in a box of white
That lies beneath the sod.

A little mouth of kisses sweet,
Two arms that hugged me tight,
Are lying quietly, safe from harm,
Beneath the sod tonight.

Oh little one, with golden curls,
Your soul is safe with God,
And may your body rest in peace.
Just underneath the sod.

DUNBAR

You sighed and men and maidens wept,
  So near them was your heart.
You sang, and to this earth a bit
  Of heaven did impart.
You laughed and hearts cast care aside
  To join you in your glee.
You mourned and many hearts bowed down,
  To grieve a while with thee.

And when at last your lovely soul
  So quietly said goodbye,
The whole world knew, and knowing
  Heaved a sad and mournful sigh.
There in your home of rest, sweet rest,
  So very far from here,
Now when you sing your tender strains,
  The angels all draw near.

And their harps they cease to string,
  Stir they not, no not a wing
"Sing," they say, "Oh poet sing,
  Sing, beloved Dunbar."

LONGING FOR MOTHER

When the world seems all against you
An' you're miles an' miles from home,
When you've just about lost courage,
An' you're sad an' all alone,—
Then you think about the old friends
That you had some time or other,
An' there's one that sets you longin'
          An' that's Mother.

An' somehow you don't take int'rest
In a thing but thoughts o' home,
Why you even don't get hungry,
All your appetite is gone.
At your work you go a shirkin'
Just can't pull yourself together,
Mighty blue, an' almost crazy
          To see Mother.

Don't the nights seem long an' dreary?
An' the pillow 'neath your head,
An' the blankets edge gets damp-like,
'Count o' tears that you have shed,
You could just cry out for comfort,
But that cry you always smother,
'Cause you'r grown, but not too grown to
          Long for Mother!

MOTHERS' DAY

———

A little girl sat all alone on the street,
With hair all unkempt and dirty bare feet.
Her dress,—should you call such,—was much soiled and
      torn,
But with this poor garment, two flowers she wore.
A snowy white lily, a lovely red rose,
Ah me, what a contrast, to such dirty clothes.

Will you sell me your flowers? I asked of the maid,
She patted them fondly, then shook her wee head,
Then "No Ma'am," she said, looking sadly at me,
"'Cause these flowers, Lady, are precious to me."
Should flowers be "precious" to this ragged child?
I forced a wee cough to hide a broad smile.

"But what need have you of the flowers, child, pray?"
"Oh this, you know Lady, is dear 'Mother's Day',
You wear a white flower if mother is dead,
And if she is living you wear one thats red.
I wish that these flowers lived always, 'cause see,
Every day's Mothers' Day, Lady, to me."

"And where is your mother," much puzzled, I said,
"You wear both the flowers, the white and the red?"
"My mother was weary and longing to rest,
So God carried her to the Land of the Blest.
She's living up there, so the minister said,
But I wear both flowers 'cause down here she's dead."

"I worked awful hard these two flowers to buy,
And I was so tired that I wanted to cry,
But I didn't, and when I was sleeping last night,

I saw my sweet mother, her face was so bright,—
She stooped down and kissed me right here on the face,
But when I awoke, I could find her no place."

"I try to be good and always I pray
To go where my mother is, Lady, some day,
And on that great day when I enter within,
Saved by Christ, and washed of all sin,
On my knees I shall thank the dear Savior and Father
And ask Him to please give me back my dear mother."

MADRE MIA

When Fortune sweetly smiles on me
And all my skies are fair,
When Love and Laughter are my guests
And I am free from care,
I then so wish that you were here,
To share my joy with me,
And sigh, O precious Mother mine,
Because it cannot be.

When little troubles gather fast,
And skies once fair are gray,
Dame Fortune comes within my grasp,
Then slips like mist away.
I need you more than ever then
To cheer my spirits low,
But deep within my lonesome heart,
I'm glad you do not know.

LOVED AND LOST

"'Tis better to have loved and lost
Than never to have loved at all."
Oh mortal, when those lines you penned
Had you drunk of the gall?
Had you then sat at twilight
Thinking while the shadows meet,
Of one you worshiped, loved and lost?
Was it not bitter sweet?
Did not your heart within you ache,
And tears unbidden fall?
Ah, mortal think, were it not best
Had you not loved at all?

FAREWELL

'Twas late we met, but ah, too soon we part,
You who are dearer to my lonely heart
   Than any I have known.
Those hours, loved one, that I spent with you
That were so pleasant dear, but ah, so few,
   Shall ever be mine own.
You came and brought with you a healing balm,
The balm of love, so soothing, sweet and calm,
   To heal my love sick heart.
And more than this, with you came hours of light
And ah, unbound my soul from sorrows night,
   My fetters tore apart.
I grieve for you, but ah, I dare not tell
To anyone but you, dear friend, farewell.

THE CALL OF LOVE

Far o'er the hills, beyond the lea,
From out the waves of restless sea
    A voice calls thee.

And far away from oceans side
O'er the green plains far and wide,
    It calls thee still.

In the forest, the nodding trees
Whisper a message for the breeze,
    To bear to thee.

The meadow flowers bend and sigh,
Birds that are mated wonder why
    You heed it not.

WE LOVE YOU JUST THE SAME

"Child," she said, "we grieve to lose you,
  Yea, our hearts are filled with pain,
But we pray that though you leave us
  May our loss be others gain.
Look to God for all your comforts
  And let heaven be your aim,
Though you are no longer with us,
  Dear, we love you just the same.

"Be an instrument for Jesus,
  Always help the fallen one;
You will find reward in heaven
  When your work on earth is done.
Often will the road be rugged
  In this world of sin and shame;
Do your best, dear child remember,
  That we love you just the same."

And on bended knees I'm praying
  That when this, my life is o'er,
I shall meet the ones that loved me
  On that bright, celestial shore.
May they stand with God the Father,
  As I cross the sullen main,
Whispering, "Though your sins were many,
  Come, we love you just the same."

REMORSE

Too late to grieve, 'tis done,
    Howl winds and death knell toll!
Just for one day of play,
    I lost my all, my soul.

Placed in the book of time,
    As countless ages roll,
"For sinful pleasures lost,
    God's gift of gifts, a soul."

With prayer I might erase,
    This charge from Time's great scroll,
But still Remorse would taunt
    "Lost just for fun, your soul!"

TO THE LAKE

———

Come, come where the breezes so gently blow,
And come when the sun in the west has sunk low,
Come love when the birdlings their homeward flights
        take
Come watch the pale moon rise on Holiday Lake.

Forget all life's cares love, come bury life's strife
Deep deep in the water, oh this love is life;
We'll dream, idly dream, while we air castles make
And drift in a skiff over Holiday Lake.

Out there on the water a boat the waves ride,
'Tis empty, and so is my life my own bride
And there in the distance, outlining the sky
Is a little grey church, with its steeple so high.

It brings happy thoughts dear, of love and of you;
I long for a cottage all cosy, for two,
Come, let us go rowing, for happy thoughts sake,
Cupid guides all the boats out on Holiday Lake.

Then come where the breezes so gently blow,
And come when the sun in the west has sunk low;
Come when the stars twinkle and tiny fires make,
Come watch the pale moon rise on Holiday Lake!

TWILIGHT DREAMS

Oft when the winter eves are closing,
While by my glowing hearth reposing
   Comes to me a vision of the past.
'Tis of man and lonely maiden,
Maid with sorrow heavy laden,
   Man with grief o'ercast.

Said the maiden, sad and lonely,
"Friend, dear friend, I care now only,
   To be numbered with the dead.
I will die by my own hand, sir,
'Tis against my Lord's command sir,
   But this life I dread.

'Tis no sin that I've committed,
Truly I have not submitted,
   To the call of foolish love.
Life for me bears no tomorrow,
That is bright, but much of sorrow,
   With dark clouds above.

Kindness I had never known
'Til you came, for you alone,
   Have been kind to me.
But tonight our paths shall sever,
For I go from earth forever,
   Friend farewell to thee."

But he seized and kissed her fiercely,
Held her tightly and she scarcely,
   Tried to pull away.
"Little girl, you cannot leave me
Can't you see? Oh, how I love thee,
   I will make you stay.

I will be your friend forever,
Your true friend and leave you never,
    I will make you glad.
I will bring you sweets and flowers,
Weave for you gay happy hours,
    You will ne'er be sad."

He to her was friend and lover,
And she longed to hold him ever,
    Fate did not permit.
Now she's wedded to another,
But she still longs for her lover,
    This she does admit.

In an easy chair reposing
Sadly musing, almost dozing,
    While the hearth fire brightly glows.
Now the maid wed to another,
Sits and dreams about her lover,
    Does he love her still? Who knows?

THE LEGEND OF THE TULIPS

The Savior of the world
Who died for you and me,
Hung bleeding, slowly dying
Upon Mount Calvary's tree.

The sun at God's command
Hid far behind the hills;
The flowers were asleep
Save one, that kept watch still.

One bright and yellow tulip
Held wide her tiny cup,
Blood trickeled from His side
And filled the wee cup up.

The flower said "My Lord,
'Tis all that I can do,
So while my sisters sleep
I hold my cup to you."

The dying Savior heard
And whispered "Little flower,
No longer yellow be
But scarlet from this hour.

And every single drop
That over flows your cup,
Within the earth shall root
And flowers red spring up.

Your little deed of love
I wish the world to know;
Bloom red, this time each year,
The time I suffered so."

Next morning when the sun
Peeped o'er Mount Calvary's head,
He saw a field of flowers,
And most of them were red.

And now throughout the earth
At Easter time, you know,
Red tulips with the yellow bloom,
Where ever tulips grow.

A CANNA LILY

The humming bird that comes
To pay me court and sips,
The dew upon my leaves
And kisses sweet my lips,
Flies to me from a far
And tells in whispers low
Of gardens lovely, fair,
Where many flowers grow.

He would that I were there
Where ferns and smilax creep,
Why should I be content
O'er window sill to peep?
Poor bird, he cannot know
What happiness is mine,
I would not change my lot
To dwell in gardens fine.

I share the sacred love
A mother gives a son,
I welcome home the sire
At eve when work is done,
I share a secret sweet
Of lovers true, and I
My head in homage bow,
When lovely maid draws nigh.

I hear the many plans
Laid for a future day,
Plans for a growing lad
Now free from care, at play.

Oftimes he quietly stands,
To gaze on me awhile,
The sire stands close beside,
Upon his face a smile.

They love my stately grace,
My gold and crimson hue,
My broad leaves gleaming bright
At early morn with dew.
They praise my beauty rare,
They love me well, I know,
Beneath this casement still
Contented I shall grow.

WE THANK THEE

———

For shelter, dear Father
  For raiment and bread,
The flowers, the trees,
  And the skies over head,
For health and for happiness
  Lent to us,—these,
For friends and for loved ones
  We bow on our knees
    And thank Thee.

The sunshine that faithfully
  Follows the rain,
The joys that we borrow
  To smother the pain,
For bright days, for dark days,
  For days that are long,
For days that are weary,
  For days filled with song,
    We thank Thee.

For love and for life,
  For the hope of a heaven,
For each precious promise
  Of thine to us given,
For time spent in labor,
  For time spent in play,
For each blessing granted
  Us day after day,
    We thank Thee.

THE LONE TREE OF THE PLAIN

Ah! marvel not that here I stand
    Upon the plain.
The old oak I, the forest king,
And in the forest deep should reign,
Where witch elm, ash, and pine trees tall,
Where silver poplar trees, and all
Pay homage grand, but here I stand
    Upon the plain.

And well I love my chosen home
    Upon the plain.
No stately subjects bow and bend
To all the plain I'm but a friend;
Amid my leaves the birds build nest
Beneath my shade the cattle rest,
How well I love my chosen home
    Upon the plain.

Then learn of me the forest king
    Upon the plain.
Be thou content what ere thy fate,
Be pleased to serve, the least is great,
When thou hast helped this world to cheer,
Be thou the subject or the peer,
Learn this of me, the forest king,
    Upon the plain.

DREAMING

I dreamed of a tiny cottage
  On a cliff above the sea,
That you had built, my darling one,
  For only you and me.
With a lovely little garden,
  Where sweetest flowers grew,
Where birdies sang a sweet refrain
  And soothing zyphers blew.

We often scampered down the cliff,
  To sit beside the sea,
And watch the billows as they danced,
  Upon the sands in glee.
And once the waves washed on the shore
  A shell all pink and wee,
You bade me hold it to my ear
  And hear it sing to me.

I dreamed we sat at even tide
  Upon a verdant crest,
To watch the great sun kiss the sea,
  Then slowly sink to rest.
We watched the pale moon shyly rise,
  All lovely; silvery green,
We saw her smile, then blush and hide
  Behind a cloudy screen.

I was the "Maid of Idleness,"
  With you my handsome knight
And naught to do but live and laugh,
  And love, from morn till night.
T'was but a dream; but such a dream,
  My treasure long shall be
To have you near me even thus,
  Is dear as life to me.

WHO'S TO BLAME?

I don't no' who to blame fo' it
   De party or de weather,
I gess de bes' t'ing I kin do
   Is name dem bofe together.

Anna Lawson gib a party,
   "Dere'll be cards," she said, "So cum,"
Now I mind yo', I aint braggin',
   But I mak's a whist game hum.

It had sno'ed dat day outrageous,
   But who keers about a sno',
An' my heart sang, "Dere'll be fun man,
   Dike yo'sef' all up an' go."

So I put my Sunday suit on
   An' my bes' an' only shoes,
Off I struts to dis here party,
   "Ole sno', sno' on, if yo' choose.

Whut I keer about yo' fallin'
   Bank on up, plum to my knee,
Yo' wid all yo' pretty whiteness,
   Yo' cain't put no skeer on me.

Yo' cain't keep me frum dat party
   Where de gals in splendor glows,
Tain't but one thing yo' kin do suh,
   Mister snow dats wet my clothes."

Bime by I reached de party,
   We played whist to points of seven,
I lost so, dat I quit playin'
   Said good night at half past 'leven.

Home I puts out, thu de sno' storm,
  Sno' a meltin' on my clothes,
Wind a whuppin' frum all angles,
  Honestly, I lak' to froze.

Den at las' I reach my shanty,
  Feet so cold I t'ink deys dead,
Puts my wet shoes in de oven
  Ob de stove an' goes to bed.

Now my mammy don't disturb me
  When I been out late at night,
So she's up nex' mo'nin' early,
  Fo' I no'd hit wus daylight.

An' I hits de flo' at seben,
  An' den much 'ginst my desire,
Off I hurries to de kitchen
  In de stove's a red hot fire.

Quick I looks in to de oven,
  Dere dey is, lo an' behol',
All de shoes I own on dis earf,
  Lay dere burnt in to a coal.

Now who's I gwine to blame fo' it,
  De party or de weather,
Gess de bes' t'ing I kin do,
  Is blame dem bofe together.

LINCOLN AND THE SOUTHLAND

Dark was the cloud that drooped over the Southland,
  Dark was the Southland as Egypt of old,
Slaves from the shores of the sunny Ethiopia,
  Like unto cattle were bargained and sold.
Women and men, little innocent children,
  Much did they suffer and long did they toil,
And by the torturing lashes persuaded,
  Turned into riches the South's fertile soil.

Torture and sorrow held sway in the Southland,
  Loud rang the snap of the torturing lash,
Hear the poor slaves as they cry loud for mercy,
  Seamed are their backs, seamed with many a gash.
Hungy and fainting, so sad and so weary,
  Bruised, beat, and battered, still toiling they go,
Listen! they sing, can they really be happy?
  Nay, but their singing gives surcease from woe.

Hear now a pitiful moan in the Southland,
  Hear now a wailing, a cry of distress,
Hear now a slave mother begging and pleading,
  While her own loved one is torn from her breast.
Torn from her breast to be sold to a stranger,
  "I will be kind," is the promise he gave,
Great is the doubt in the heart of the mother,
  But speak, she dare not, for she is a slave.

What if a mother be torn from her loved ones,
  She gave them birth, but dare claim them her own,
Nay, they are slaves and belong to her master,
  Ah, cruel master, his will must be done.
What if a sister be torn from a brother,
  What if a husband be torn from a wife,
Why should he grieve, can he not find another,
  Why cling to one woman all of one's life?

Hear now the sound coming out of the swampland,
  That is the yelp of thé master's blood hound,
Some weary slave has escaped from his fetters,
  Woe be unto him if he should be found.
Great the reward for his capture is offered,
  Dead or alive,—it were better he die,
Than to return to the bonds of his master,
  Better by far in the swampland to lie.

Long had they prayed, these the slaves of the Southland,
  Prayed in their agony, year after year,
Prayed without ceasing, and never once doubting
  That God the Father would answer their prayer.
"God who delivered the children of Israel,
  Turn not a deaf ear on this, our plea,
Help us, oh merciful God, for we perish,
  Send us deliverance, Lord set us free."
And came a man with his heart filled with pity,

  Sorrow and grief had been stamped on his face,
And he spoke fearlessly, pleading that justice
  Be given unto a much abused race.
Spoke he not meekly, in sweet scented phrases,
  Carefully coating in honey each word,
But like the peal of the deep rolling thunder,
  He spoke, and spoke frankly; all the world heard.

"These are thy brothers," said he to the Southland,
  "Why should ye bind them with fetter and chain?
Why should ye sell them like so many cattle?
  Women and men sold for gold,—paltry gain.
Loose ye, oh Southland, your chains and your fetters,
  Let them go forth and be men among men,
Let them abide by the same laws that bind you,
  And let Old Glory, their welfare defend."

He who his hands might have washed, and like Pilate,
  Said, "Bear ye witness of this, I am clean,"
Plead with a heart filled with fire for a nation,
  Plead and was guided by powers unseen.

Bitter his enemies, great his oppressors,
   But he stood firmly, fearful of none,
Firm as a mountain, with spirit untrammeled,
   He stood for the right and standing thus won.

Banished the cloud that drooped over the Southland,
   Wailings and groans now give place to a song,
Grateful Ethiopia is thanking the Father
   For the brave Lincoln that righted the wrong.
Engrave his name on the great scroll of ages,
   For a just cause he his life sacrificed,
Earth has recorded his deeds and proclaims him
   Greatest of men since the day of Christ.

OLD FLAG FOR MY PEOPIE AND YOU

———

Black was his face
As the wings of the raven,
And he lay dying.
Black, but a soul
That the angels are praising
And men glorifying.
"Stick to the flag, Boy,"
His captain had ordered.
He obeyed the order
When his right hand
From the arm had been severed;
He held with the other.

Now on his cot
The black hero is lying,
Suffering but smiling.
There at the foot
Of his cot hangs Old Glory,—
For her he is dying.
"Nurse, put that flag please
'Round my cold shoulders,"
Smiling he said,
"I've something to tell her,
Hope she remembers it
After I'm dead."

"Old flag"—hear him whisper,
"For you I am dying,
But then it is well,
Out there 'neath the gray skies
My comrades are lying,
Amid shock and shell,

And my people, O flag,
Are on bended knees praying
All over the world.
Pleading for mercy
My cruel injustices
At them are hurled.

"For you we have fought
And 'tis you we are trusting.
Flag, promise me then,
That henceforth wherever
Your stripes wave, my brothers
Be treated as men.
Our blood has flowed freely
To make this, your red stripe.
We've stood brave and true,
Your white our purity,
Blue, our loyalty,—
Ah! We've been true blue.

"When gray clouds of grim war
No longer shall hover,
All over the world
And you free from blood stain
And grime of the battle
In peace are unfurled,
Think then, how we pressed on
Weak, footsore, and wounded
The victory to win.
Then say to the world,
    'My bars will protect them.'
For they have been men.

"Make away with the stake,
Forget rope and tree,
Let Justice step in,
Let your stars, and your bars,
Protect my black brothers.
Flag, wipe out the sin!

I've loved you, I've served you,
I've fought to protect you,
Dear red, white and blue,
Remember, O pride of my heart,
That I die for
My people, and you."

THE VAMPIRE

———

**Now this is the story she told me
When I went to her preaching "Reform,"
'Tis a story, so true, never old, never new,
Let me tell you, 'twill do you no harm.**

"A vampire you call me, a fiend sent from Hell
   To suck the life blood from your men, it is well
That you hail me thus, think of me as you may,
   I laugh as my fiddle of heart strings I play.
With rosin of hatred I polish my bow,
   The tune is 'Revenge' that I'm playing so slow,
The strings break, I laugh, as I cast them aside,
   I then tune up new ones and let my bow slide.

"I've wrecked many homes with my satanic smile,
   I grieve o'er my own folly once in awhile,
My own soul looks down on my life in disgust,
   My conscience says sometimes to me, 'Tis not just
To play with the heartstrings of lives in this way'.
   But 'twould please me to know that I helped in some
I tell you 'tis man, do you dare disagree?
   If so tell me why, and then listen to me.

"My faith in man placed me in this evil way,
   My hatred for men now demands here I stay.
I loved with a fervor death only could break,
   For this Fate repaid me one endless heartache.
As I play with the heartstrings of love-hungry men,
   I forget for awhile my own sorrow, but when
Dame Memory bids me recall, dream and think,
   I drain sorrows cup to the dregs, bitter drink.

"Men blind us with love, and then lead us to shame
And we cast to the four winds our all, a good name.
When I think of the poor souls that lie in a grave,
And the wretches like me that no heaven can save,
I would that the power of satan were mine,
And I'd crush souls of men until end of the time.
Vengence is God's, and I know he'll repay,
But 'twould please me to know that I helped in some
way.

"You think me severe in my judgment of man,
But deny as the truth my one word, if you can!
Then think of countless maids, innocent, pure,
That fell trusting blindly, that man would be true.
Go purge out the beast, that abides in your men,
The vampire and wanton will lose her place then.
Men learned or illiterate, great men or small
Hold one thing common,—he is brute after all.

"The men whom the laws of your city enforce
You deem to be honest, as matter-of-course,
Your judges, your lawyers, your sheriffs and more
Of your city officials, pass through my door.
Why visit they me then? Your state laws demand
That none of my type be allowed in the land.
Most all men are traitors? Then say if you can,
Whom God will condemn most, the vampire or man?"

"The husband and father, whose babies and wife
Make life well worth living, soon tires of that life
So restless and weary, and longing to play,
To the haunt of the vampire, he soon hies his way,
To forget lifes great trial, to live for awhile
The life that enthralls him, while I lie and smile,
When to satisfaction, his lust has been fed
He pays with the price of his little ones bread."

"The minister, God's chosen one, so you say
  Who is pointing this vile world the heavenly way,
Knocks soft at my chamber, on dark stilly night,
  With voice filled with passion, implores that he might
Shed his garb of mock purity, just for a time
And his Sunday collections, God's money, is mine!
His plea is, 'I'm human,—a flesh and blood man,
  None need know I come here, so charge me none can.'

"I smile sweetly smile, as I tell him his hair
  Lies in beautiful waves, when there's not a wave there!
I then praise his stature, his voice or his eyes,
  I flatter him much with my beautiful lies.
I tell him that life ne'er before was so sweet
  And fate surely willed it, that we two should meet.
He pays a big price for the sweet things I say,
  The more that I flatter, the more he will pay.

"The peacock struts proudly, his feet wound his pride,
  The moon will at times behind clouds, shyly hide,
But, man, that vain creature, stands perfect alone,
  To judge, but admits to no faults of his own!
And should the world know of his sins, small or great,
  The fact 'twas a man, clears the charge from time's
          slate,
But I am a woman, a vampire, and see
  The hypocrites all point a finger at me!

"I'm branded without, and a deep scar within
  Bleeds on, as I play with the heartstrings of men,
And bleed on it shall until Death and I meet,
  Then a life stained and tainted, I'll lay at his feet.
And when at the judgment, condemned I shall stand,
  With my victims around me, like grains of the sand,
Which of my accusers will 'cast the first stone?'
  Not one, for they all, for some sin must atone.

"A vampire you call me, a fiend sent from Hell!
  Your charge I deny not, but oh, let me tell.
The tune I am playing is sweet to my ears,
  To others, perhaps, it means sorrow and tears.
Men furnish the strings and then pay me to play,
  The strings break, I laugh as I cast them away!
With rosin of hatred I polish my bow,
  The tune is 'Revenge' that I'm playing so slow."

ENCOURAGEMENT

'Twas just a tiny word of praise,
  Perhaps 'twas idly given,
But, ah, it bade me onward press
Through disappointments and distress,
'Twas but a word, but ah, that word
  Gave me a peep at Heaven.

A PRAYER

Lord, I am weak, and weaker do
I seem to grow each day.
Grant, grant me strength, O Lord of Host,
And guide me on I pray.

The tempter calls, and bargains for
This soul of mine each day.
I must not heed him, Lord, dear Lord,
Give strength, more strength I pray.

How often Lord, how oft I grope
In darkness for the day;
Sun of my soul, light up this path
Of gloom I tread, I pray.

WHERE IS THE LAND?

———

Wind of the east as you scamper and play,
Cease from your frolics and sing me a lay,
Sing of a land where the sweet.flowers grow,
A land made for souls that no sorrows know,
A land of much happiness, sunshine and bliss,
A land of affection, the Island of Kiss,
Surrounded by waters, the waters of youth,
And governed by wise men, Faith, Honor and Truth.
If you have not found it, you may some glad day,
Oh wind, when you find it, come show me the way!

WEARY

Gamble, gamble, life's a chance,
  So play and be merry.
Death is partner in the dance
  Of the weary, weary.

Gain and loss, loss and gain,
  Sunshine days and dreary,
Death will some day ease the pain,
  Of the weary, weary.

SOCIETY

———

Where all the bad is counted good,
And all the right is wrong;
Where gossip is the chief asset
And slander floats in song.
Where chaperons need guides themselves,
Where virtuous maids are rare;
Where men win hearts and then break hearts,
Without a thought or care.
Where baby is a bother now
Instead of love and joy,
A little doggie takes its place,
"He's such a darling toy."
Where every body tries to be
Most popular in the set,
And win that title dear to them
"The social circle's pet."
Where gold and jewels are the gods,
Forgotten piety.
Now sum it up, the answer is,
Our great society!

A FRIEND WAS NEEDED

If ever mortal needed friend,
  A kind and helping hand to lend,
'Twas then, when all things seemed to turn
  Around and 'round, and temples burn,
And throb nigh unto bursting,
  The little empty phial I have,
And I shall keep it, 'tis a treasure,
  And you, a true friend, I shall hold
In memory's chest, so safe, with pleasure!

TEARS AND CARESSES

I begun a letter with tears
But ended it with a kiss;
The kiss for the love I hold for my dear,
And tears for that dear one I miss.

A few tears, a few sweet caresses,
Fills life's little year after year,
May the tears all be followed by kisses;
The kisses to blot out the tears.

GRIEVE NOT THE SPIRIT

On bended knees I prayed
    That love divine
Fill to o'er flowing this
    Vile heart of mine.
So earnestly I prayed
    The Lord did hear,
And answered me according
    To my prayer.

His Holy Spirit came
    With me to dwell;
Great joy was mine then thinking
    All was well.
Soon I forgot to praise my God
    Or pray,
And sorely grieved, the Spirit
    Would not stay.

And to replace that love that
    Once abound,
Within my soul, I searched
    The earth, but found
Not anything with that love
    To compare.
Though now I pray, God answers
    Not my prayer.

WHO AM I?

And who am I, that God should be
So very merciful to me!
I, who once laughed to scorn the way
Of Holiness, refused to pray.
Nay, let the poor unlettered soul,
Go moaning, praying, to the goal,
Not I, what vain, what hollow thing
From morn till night to pray and sing!
So proud, so vain, so wordly-wise,
Self righteous scales had sealed my eyes.

But not, thank God, 'twas his good pleasure,
To bless me with a priceless treasure.
O, holy love, O love divine,
And Holy Spirit, mine, all mine!
The Veil of Doubt in twain is torn,
And peeping through, I see the morn.
Bright morn of life's eternal day,
And once I laughed to scorn this way!
Yea, who am I that God should be
So very merciful to me?

I AM NAUGHT

For I am naught but God indeed
Calms every fear, fills every need.
And when the way seems dark and drear
He whispers gently, "I am near,
Press on, for though thy strength is small
I'll lend thee aid, thou shalt not fall,
And when thy body racks with pain
Need thou but call upon my name,
A great physician I will be
To all who put their faith in me.

I'll keep thee from the tempter's snare,
I'll share with thee thy every care,
With thee I'll walk and talk each day,
If thou my statutes wilt obey.
I'll be thy comforter, and friend,
And when thy life on earth shall end
A home in heaven I shall give,
O soul, where thou shalt ever live."
A speck of vile humanity
Am I, and God does this for me!

THEY KNOW NOT

My life is sad,
But no one knows
But my soul and I.
I often weep
And heave a sigh,
But dry my tears
When friends draw nigh,
And sing a lay!

WHICH?

———

One gave me all
    That was in his power!
    One gave me naught
But heart aches and sorrow!
    Which love I most?

TO THE GRADUATE

———

May God abide with you throughout life's journey,
  And keep you safely from the Tempter's snare,
All joys be thine, my little friend, and only,
  The best that life may offer be your share.
And should the cares of life around you gather
  And trouble's fetters seem to hold you fast,
Pray, little friend, and as you pray remember
  The sun shines brighter, when the cloud has passed.

OLD YEAR YOU'RE DYING CONFESS

Old year you're dying,
So slowly so slow.
Why not confess to
The world 'ere you go.
Tell us your secret,
Your joy and your woe;
Tell us the things that
You only can know.
Old year you're dying
    Confess.

TO RUTH RAY

———

Things aren't the same
Dear since you came,
Skies are more blue above,
The once sad earth
Doth burst with mirth
And love is more than love.

This life so sweet
Grows more complete,
Each day of every seven,
Your coming dear
Brought to us here,
A little bit of Heaven.

A CHURCH CONFERENCE

I has called dis bo'ad togedder
  Wid yo' members, so dat we
Co'ld cull out some sheep not wanted in dis fol'.
  No chu'ch won't 'mount to nuffin',—
Yo' kin tak' dis much f'um me,—
  Wid a lot ob ole bac' biters on de rol'.
So tonite I'se on inspectshun
  An' I'se gw'ine a-clean de fo'te
I'se gw'ine a cast out debils,—
  Brother Clerk, read yo' rep'ote!

"Brazos Bottom, Texas,
  Nite ob Januwerry eight,
In dis year ob our Lawd nineteen an' fo',
  De Hard Shell Baptist
Held a conf'runce on the jus' said date.
  'Twas de fust one ob de blessed year, yo' no.
Fust we had sum glor'ous singin'
  Followed by a word ob prayer,
Den de min'ets whut I rote las' time wus read.
  De pastor made a few remarks
About a glad New Year,
  But I don't remember ev'ryt'ing he said.
We den got down to bissness,
  But we didn't quite git thru,
So de bissness wus pos'pon'ded 'till nex' month.
  Wid all my heart declar'in'
Dat de min'ets read is true,
  I'se yo' humble secaterry,
            Brother Blunt."

"If yo' fin' deres no objections
  Den de min'ets stand approved,

Since dere be none we will now get down to fac's.
　Fust t'ing, deres sum deacons
On dis b'oad dat mus' be moved,
　Fo' six months or mo' I'se been out on dey trac's.
Wait,—is ev'ry body in dis house
　A member ob dis chu'ch?
If yo' ain't, den will yo' kindly hit de do'?
We don't mean to hurt yo' feelin's,
Be us fur removed f'um such,
　But dis meetin's fo' us Baptist folks yo' no.

Brother Mitchell, dat means yo' too,
　'Cause yo' don't b'long to dis chu'ch,
Dey has got yo' name down on de rol' I no,
　But yo' nebber has been burried
In de water, in as much
　As yo ain't—well den I gess yo' better go."
"Well, whut is hit, Brother Hooper?"
　"Brother pastor, hits a shame
An' I makes a move dat Brother Mitchell stay.
　If yo' no'd he weren't no member
Ob dis chu'ch why in de name
　Ob de stars above did yo' accept his pay?"

"Has airry one objections
　To de move de brother made?"
"Yes, I has," "Alright, Sis Johnson hab yo' say."
　"Hits jus' dis, de rules and by-rules
Ob dis chu'ch is made an' laid
　An' yo' don't becum' a member 'cause yo' pay."
"All who 'grees to brother Mitchell
　Stayin' in dis conf'runce here
Kindly stan' upon yo 'feet an' let us no,—
　Only five, the nays so hab it
So to me hit do appear,
　Brother Mitchell dat dey means fo' yo' to go."

"Now fust upon dis lis' I has
　Is Deacon Ellis Green.

Green, dey tell me yo' done gone an' talk'd too much,
  An' f'um rep'otes I gether
Yo' done tol' de folks outside,
  Whuts been goin' wid de money ob de chu'ch.
I's not gwine to ask de deacons
  Whuts dey pleasure in dis case,
An' I don't keer whether dey is pleased or no',
  Yo' done ruint my repertashun
Yo' done put me in disgrace,
  An' I'se turned yo' out, so git yo' hat an' go.'

"Well, alright, dere Sister Mitter,
  Seems as if yo' has de flo',
Speak right out, whut has yo' got to say?"
  "Brother pastor, hits jus' dese few words:
In all my life befo'
  I ain't nebber seed no one turn'd out dat way.
I'se been in dis Baptist chu'ch now
  Putty nigh on thirty years,
An' I no's its rules and by-laws ev'ry one."
  "I object,"—"Sit down Sis Mitter,
I is runnin' t'ings 'round here,
  An' all t'ings mus' hab dey fust time to be done."

"De nex' one on dis lis' I has
  Is deacon Luther White.
Fo' a long time White's been tryin' to run me down.
  Now he's done got a petition
Whut a lot ob yo' done signed,—
  Dis petition is to get me out ob town.
Deacon White, dis chu'ch don't need yo',
  So I's gwine to scratch yo' name,
An' I'se got de names ob all whut signed yo' lis',
  But I feel to turn de po' souls out
Would sorter be a shame,
  So yo'll set still an' lissun good to dis."

"Mos' ob yo' whut signed dat paper
  Ain't got nary right to vote;

'Cause yo' way behind, I'll mind yo' in yo' dues,
    An' yo' vote would be es heavy
Es a feather on a goat,—
    Set down dere brother Huggins, I refuse
Fo' to lissun to yo' right now
    Don't yo' see I'se got de flo'?
Cain't yo' wait 'til I'se thru talkin'?
    If yo' cain't, yo' better go."

"When yo' called me fo' to cum here
    Dis here chu'ch had gone to rack,
An' de members wus all scattered fur an' near,
    Now deys lot of new ones jine us
All de ole ones done cum back,
    So yo' thru wid me, an' wants me way fum here.
Well, I tell yo', I ain't gwine;—
    I has cum right here to stay,
An' right here de Lawd will fin' me
    When he call me Jedgment day."

"We has spent much time in talkin'
    An' I'se f'aid we won't git thru
'Cause already now de time is mos' nigh spent,
    An' we ought to go on home right now,
But deres another one
    Dat I mus' turn out, so I kin be content,
An' dats Sister Mamie Tripple,
    Who is spreadin' it dat I
Has been flirtin' wid de young gals of dis fol'.
    Now dat rumor bares no truth a tall,
An' I is won'drin, why
    Sister Tripple sech a tale as dat has tol'.
Now Chu'ch I is not guilty,
    An' yo' has no right to b'leive—"

"Brother pastor, do yo' dare to say I lies?
    I'se got witness here to prove it
Dat yo' kissed young Annie Reeves,

An' deys right here now a lookin' in yo' eyes.
An' I'se got sum other secrets
  If I choose, I could expose
So yo' better cut yo' cards an' deal 'em slow.
  I'se aquainted wid de party
Dat gib yo' dat suit ob clothes,
  But I isn't gwine to call her name out do'
I could tell dis conjergation
  Where yo' got dat Stetson hat,
But I'se not a callin' names, so don't yo' fear.
  An' dat diamond pin yo' wearin'
I no's jus' who give yo' dat,
  An' de lady is a settin' right in here.

"When yo' ask a month to res' up
  An' 'tend lac' yo's gwine away
I can tell dis conjergation whut yo' did.
  Yo' stayed right here in dis Bottom
An' I no jus' whar yo' stay,
  An' I no de very house in which yo' hid.
Den yo' tell dis conjergation
  Dat I'se spreadin' tales untrue,
Yo' done got my blood a bilin' an' I'se mad,
  If I tell all dat I's no'in',
Dese men folks would murder yo'
  An' I'se here to say dat wouldn't be too bad."

"Sit down, sit down, sister Tripple,
  Yo' is out ob order now,"—
"Out ob order? Well I don't keer if I am.
  I'se gwine let dis conjergation no,
An' let it no jus' how
  Dey done choose a wolf an' thought dey had a lamb.
I could tell 'em—"Sit down, sister,
  Sit down, 'til I hab a say,
An' my say is dis, I'se gwine to resign,
  Why I wouldn't stay amongst such folks
As yo'll a nother day,
  I is leavin' here tonite on number nine!"

AFTER WHILE

———

A little while to wait and then
The mystic veil of Time shall rend
   And I shall see and understand.
Death gently will the veil divide
And bid my soul come rest abide
   Forever in a happy land.

THUS

As the days have passed
Today soon will follow,
What will the Fates mete
Unto us tomorrow?
                    Thus we live.

True friends and loved ones
Stand 'round about and weep,
Tired eyelids closed
In a never wakening sleep.
                    Life is o'er.

CREEDS

The church grows more like Babylon
   As these vile years roll slowly on,
And are these truly sent by God
   Who through the Bible plow and plod,
To find on which to base their creed
   One word, then bid the whole world heed?

I dare not judge, oh Lord of Host
   I stand confused, like traveler lost
Far from the road on darksome night
   Shall I turn left, shall I turn right!
Or shall I sit down by the way,
   And calmly wait for night and day?

The church grows more like Babylon,
   As these last years roll slowly on,
New doctrines are born each day
   New creeds that point a novel way
To God, confused, we do not know
   What to believe; which way to go.

A PRAYER

———

Yielding to temptation
More and more each day;
Growing weak and weary,
Help me Lord, I pray.

Like unto the driftwood,
Drifting from the shore,
Drifting with the current,
Lost forever more.

Soul and mind and body,—
All are vile with sin.
And I pray thee, Father,
Cleanse without, within.

LINES

And Fate has bade me
    Hope and wait
And bury my sorrow in song!
    I sing and hope,
But Fate, oh Fate,
    Have I not waited long?

A CHILD'S MUSING

I wonder if the lilies know
  About the Lord, who suffered so!
I wonder if the birds that sing
  Know the message Easter brings!
And when at night, I kneel to pray
  To Him who guides me night and day!
I wonder how it chanced to be
  That He should die for you and me?

LINES

———

'Tis but a little we're seeking,
   But seeking the little seems vain.
Year after year, we go toiling,
   Time lends less joy and more pain.

Weary and worn after toiling,
   Filled with remorse after play,
Shall we find bliss in the morning,
   When Time is no more? Who can say?

LINES

Some day you'll come back to me,
   Come back some day I know,
Some day, dear heart, your face I'll see
   For love has told me so.
Some day you'll heed loves' pleading call
   Now falling on deaf ears.
Some day you'll claim me, all and all,
   Some day in after years.

YOU TOO?

And can it be that you whom I did cherish,
As my true friend, so soon have weary grown,
You who once leaned to catch my every murmur,
My every song in sad or merry tone?
And now without one mite of warning given
The stream of cold indifference flows wide,
Friend, which of us will brave the chilly waters
To reach the other on the distant side?

A friendship bought, a friendship hastily chosen,
Divides and leaves a chasm of disgust,
True friendship tied with strong cords of devotion
Are, Oh so often severed by mistrust.
The friends of our own flesh, our even kindred,
Oft turn aside, nor heed our pleading cry,
All this I know, but still somehow it grieves me
That we grew disconcerted, you and I.

Ah, friend of mine, you too, like many others
Of friendship pure and honest weary grew,
'Tis strange what tricks our fancies play upon us,
So oft we seek the false, cast off the true.
But, Ah, methinks that somewhere in the future,
Before this course, this weary race is run,
Dame memory will bid us long for old friends,
As traveler lost at night longs for the sun.

JUST DREAMS

Dreams in sweet childhood
    Of fairies and goblins,
Dreams and air castles
    'Mid school books and toys,
Dreams when a maiden
    Of gay knights and lovers,
Dreams, happy dreams
    Void of griefs, only joys.

Dreams of a life mate
    And cozy wee cottage,
Of course not too tiny,
    But just the right size,
Dreams then of motherhood
    Far best, the sweetest,
Wondering what color
    Will be the baby's eyes.

Dreams of the future
    For mother's own darling,
Hoping that all things
    For him will be bright,
Thus are the dreams
    Of life's spring, summer, autumn,
Morn, noonday and evening,
    But what of the night?

The night and the winter
    When life is all hoary,
The sunshine is fading
    The future obscure.
Waiting, just waiting
    With naught but the memories
Of dreams that were sweet
    But so seldom came true.

SUFFERING LOVE

I cannot say that you my friend surprise me,
    Long have I known that you must speak some day,
My heart responds to all your love and passion,
    But ah, convention bids me say you nay.

Your sigh fell on mine ear when I drew near you,
    Your face flushed and grew brighter when I spake,
I loved you and I knew you loved me madly,
    But love must suffer for convention's sake.

Convention bids me lie when I am longing,
    To heed the call of Love that thrills my frame,
Once all was fair in love but times are changing,
    And even Love now plays a losing game.

I dare not stroll with you as 'tis your bidding,
    At twilight or when shadows gather deep,
We dare not go and sit beside the river
    When all the world save lovers are asleep.

I dare not listen to your mad "I-love-yous"
    Or gaze at length into your love lit eyes,
Dear, I would nestle in your arms and kiss you,
    Convention whispers, "It would not be wise."

This soulless world of poise and much pretention,
    Has stamped a lie on even Cupid's face,
A few have souls, he whom this gift possesses,
    Must crush and hide it as 'twere some disgrace.

It grieves me that I cannot heed your pleadings,
    'Tis true I love you and my heart will ache,
But we must wear the mask and go on groping,
    With laden hearts, dear, for convention's sake.

WAITING

———

I count time no longer by days nor by weeks,
    Nor months, but by slow rolling years,
My eyes that once sparkled with youth and with love,
    Are often now blinded by tears.
The years roll so slowly, my heart is so full,
    Of sighs that give no place to song,
Come back to me dear, I have waited, am waiting,
    Will wait, but Oh darling, how long!

WHAT DO WE WANT?

————

Hear my prayer, Lord, and let it rain,
A mortal pleads, once and again.
　Rain Lord, please let there be.
The drought is parching all the grain,
The cattle dying on the plain,
　Dear Lord, please send the rain.

And it did rain for many a day,
I heard this self same mortal say:
　Dear Lord, please stop the rain.
The floods have washed our barns away,
The harvest fields in ruin lay,
The lightning kills the stock each day,
　Dear Lord, stop the rain, I pray.

STILL THERE IS LOVE

The Fates look down upon us
  With a frown that makes us twitch,
By prejudice is barred each son of Ham.
  We are much abused and scoffed at
By the poorest and the rich,
  In our face the law the doors of Justice slam.
But life is not all darkness,
  Though through darkness oft we rove,
'Tis proven, naught that burdens us
  Can rob our souls of love.

We love the spring time flowers,
  And the sunny days of June,
With its cooling fragrant zyphers that blow by
  The robin in the tree top
Sings to us his sweetest tune,
  The rainbow still makes beautiful the sky
We forget our songs of sorrow,
  When we hear the moaning dove,
Fate has not, cannot rob us of
  That gift from Heaven, Love.

IN MY EVENING AFTER WHILE

———

Shall my life be just as happy
　In the evening of my day,
As it was in my life's morning,
　As it is at noon now, pray?
Shall I look beyond the shadows
　That are sure to come, and smile,
Will Love be my guest, I wonder?
　In my evening after while!

LINES

Weary of sins and temptations that haunt me,
  Weary of fighting the same sin each day,
Failing to be what the Savior would have me,
  Groping although he has shown me the way.

Pilate and Peter and Judas together,
  Could not have caused him more sorrow, I know
Have I not tried Him, denied Him, betrayed Him,
  Thoughts of my follies o'erwhelm me with woe.

Lord, I am grieved with my sinful behavior,
  Prone at thy feet in repentance I lie,
Cleanse, and forgive, I implore thee kind Savior,
  Cleanse me of all sin and then let me die.

THE CHOSEN ONE

One offered me gold
　And much luxury;
One offered me fame,
　A famous man, he.
One offered adventure,
　All offers seem droll!
So I choose the poet,
　He gave me a soul!

I WONDER

If God should call me on that one great day
To answer for my past and to me say:
"What didst with the talents I gave thee,
Oh soul, that I so honored, answer me?
Didst thou use them, the sad old earth to cheer,
To help it smile, while thou didst tarry there?"

Should I make answer, "Lord I did not know
Thou wouldst have me use the talents so
I was afraid to displease Thee, so I,
Laid them away, in dust and rust they lie."
Then shall I hear Him say, "O soul, well done,
Come and receive the crown that thou hast won!"
                    I wonder?

JASPER RAY

'Cose I no he's mighty sticky
　　Wid dese 'lasses on his hands,
But dis sticky mouf an' fingers
　　Mak's him sweeter,—goodness lands.
Why dis wurld would not be jus' so
　　If hit wus'nt fo' dis chile!
See dem purty eyes a sparklin'
　　See dem teef? Ain't dat sum smile?
Whut I keer if he is sticky!
　　Hab a right to be dat way,
An' yo' daddy loves yo' better
　　When yo' sticky, Jasper Ray.

Dere's nights when I'se so tired
　　Dat I mos' nigh needs a prop,
Fo' to put between my shoulders
　　So's to hol' me les' I drop.
My po' feet is so' an' swollen,
　　Dere's a achin' thru my ches'
I is jus' wo' out all over
　　An' Lo'd no's I need a res'.
So I sets down in my rocker,—
　　It has been one try'in' day,—
Here he cum an' clamb all on me,
　　Jus a grinin', Jasper Ray!

Den he'll ask me sweet as honey,
　　"Ain't yo' workin' jus' fo' me?"
An' I says, "I sho' is, honey,"
　　Den he'll say, "Well, let me see
How much money yo' got fo' me,
　　Tell me jus' how much yo' mak'."
So I han' him one whole dollar,
　　'Cause I no dats whut hit takes,

An' instid ob sayin' "Thanky"
   He jus' hug me tight and say:
"My I sho' does love yo' daddy,
   Does yo' love yo' Jasper Ray?"

Den he tell me all whut happened
   'Round de whole house since I lef',
An' he tell on ev'ry body,
   But he sho' leave out his self.
So I say, "Whut yo' been doin'
   All day long, Ole Button Eye?"
"Daddy bet yo' sho' been naughty."
   Den he chune all up to cry.
'Tendin' lac' he been o'fended
   'Cause I call him names, he say,
But he wants to change de subjec'
   An' he wins, too, Jasper Ray.

He kin sho' ask heap o' questions
   An' las' night to me he say:
"Daddy, tell me how cum granny
   All day long jus' sing an' pray?
An' how cum she holler 'Glory'
   An' shake ev'ry body's han'?"
"Grandma's happy," I says, "baby,"
   But de chile don't understan'.
An' he say, "I'se always happy,
   But I sho' don't act dat way,"
"When yo' little soul finds Jesus,
   Yo'll praise God, too, Jasper Ray."

Once agin he change de subjec',—
   "Oh, I seed a man today
Whut had jus' one foot an' two sticks,
   An' he walk lac' dis away."
Den he jump down fo' to sho' me
   An' he hop along de flo',
Slow an' painful-like an' keerful
   Lac' a cripple man fo' sho'.

I jus' hated fo' to stop him,
   'Cause hit made his heart so gay,
But I warns, "God would not hab yo'
   Mock de cripples, Jasper Ray."

"Sing a song fo' yo' daddy,"
   An' dat little voice ob love,
Floats in silver strains to heaven,
   An' de angels up above
Stoop to listen to dat baby,
   Singin' "If yo' keep de faith,"
Why I wants to go to Glory,
   Right now, I don't want to wait.
An' de entire house gits silent
   Dat boy no's he's holdin' sway,
Wid dat precious voice ob hissen,
   Keep on singin', Jasper Ray.

After whil' his song is ended,
   An' he 'gin to nod his head,
So I calls out to his mammy;
   "Ella, fix dis buggahs' bed."
Bimeby his mammy shake me,
   An' she say, "Fo' goodness sake,
Yo an' Jasper sho' is sleepin',
   Lac' to nebber git yo' wake.
Thought yo' had de job ob keepin'
   Not ob sleepin', but I lay,
Dat yo' sleepin' even harder
   Den our little Jasper Ray."

She den wash de sticky darlin',
   Clean an' lay him on his cot;
She jus' dare me fo' to tech him,
   But she jus' as well as not.
Fo' hit seem de very debil say,
   "Now ain't dat baby sweet?"
An' mak me kiss his purty face
   An' pinch his tiny feet.

He's tired as me I reckin,
  An' ain't done a t'ing but play;
How I wish yo' life could always
  Be a playtime, Jasper Ray!

Slow I pulls de breeches kiver
  Up an' tucks hit 'neaf' his chin,
An' I tucks hit at de foot too,
  So de cold air cain't git in.
Den his mammy stan' beside me,
  An' she whisper wid a smile:
"Ain't dat little rascal growin?
  Runnin' up lac' sumt'ing wild."
Den we bofe bows down together
  At his bedside an we pray;
We thank de Lord fo' ev'ry t'ing
  But mos' fo' Jasper Ray.

AND NOW GOODNIGHT

———

I have told you tuneful tales,
Gathered from the hills and vales,
Wheresoever mine own people chanced to dwell.
If the tales have brought you mirth,
Brought more laughter to the earth,
          It is well.

For I vowed to you I could,
And I promised that I would
Sing a little lay of laughter that would rid
Thine own heart of cares awhile,
Leave upon thy face a smile,
          And I did!

notes to the introduction

1. We are indebted to the great African-American poet Mari Evans, who read and commented on the poems of Bernice Love Wiggins. Ms. Evans carefully reminded us not to think of dialect poetry in pejorative terms and other uncritical ways, and that she prefers labeling it idiom poetry. The point is, however, that black speech patterns, whether labeled as dialect or idiom, are to be taken seriously by scholars to ascertain worldviews, historical realities, and creative use of language, rather than dismissing that language usage as imperfect and inept. Gwendolyn Bennett left the state at a young age, but her girlhood in Giddings, Texas, influenced her writing, and her art, prose, and poetry sparkled within the covers of literary magazines in her day. She was the first female recipient of a Guggenheim Fellowship.

2. Trips to Los Angeles, searches in El Paso, and general birth and death records have failed to turn up any significant information on Bernice Love Wiggins and her kin. In The Texas Department of Health's Bureau of Vital Statistics there is a death certificate for Austin Love, Jr., born on March 9, 1909, and whose parents were Austin Love Sr. and Alberta Clark. This is the closest we could get to unraveling the mysteries of Bernice Love Wiggins's origins. It is possible that Austin Love Sr. may have been her father. A check of social security numbers did not produce a Bernice Love Wiggins in the records, but she may have married and obtained such a number under her new surname, assuming that she indeed lived through the late 1930s. In the early 1930s, Bernice Love Wiggins operated a kindergarten ("where the little ones work while they play") on Durazno Street in El Paso, charging ten cents a day per child. She listed herself then as Mrs. B. Love-Wiggins. For information on Bernice Love Wiggins's activities in the 1930s in El Paso, see Maceo Crenshaw Dailey, *I'm Building Me A Home: El Paso's African Ameri-*

can Community, 1539–1998 (Commemorative Black History
Month Pamphlet published by Chase Bank: El Paso, 1998).
      3. Maceo Crenshaw Dailey Jr. and Kristine Navarro, *Where-
soever My People Chance to Dwell: Oral Interviews with African
American Women of El Paso* (Black Classic Press: Baltimore,
2000), 4–14.
      4. Examples of the new and excellent literary and historical
work to reconstruct the black experience in the West are Bruce
A. Glasrud and Laurie Champion, *The African American West: A
Century of Short Stories* (Boulder: University Press Of Colorado,
2000) and Quintard Taylor, *In Search of the Racial Frontier:
African Americans in the American West, 1528–1990* (New York:
W. W. Norton & Company, 1998). Additional works that will
prove useful in the discussion of African Americans in El Paso
and the state of Texas: Alwyn Barr, *Black Texans: A History of
African Americans in Texas, 1528–1995* (Norman: University of
Oklahoma Press, 1996, 2nd Edition); Maceo Crenshaw Dailey Jr.
and Kristine Navarro, *Wheresoever My People Chance to Dwell:
Oral Interviews with African American Women of El Paso* (Baltimore: Black Classic Press, 2000); Ruthe Winegarten, *Black Texas
Women: A Sourcebook* (Austin: University of Texas Press, 1996);
and Ruthe Winegarten, *Black Texas Women: 150 Years of Trial
and Triumph* (Austin: University of Texas Press, 1995). A select-
ed bibliography, provided at the end of this book, is an additional
guide to those interested in the larger subject of African Americans as well as those who resided in Texas.

selected bibliography

Baker, Glo Dean. *I Am Woman, I Am Black*. Austin: Afro-
American Players,1978.

Barr, Alwyn. *Black Texans: A History of Negroes in Texas, 1528-
1971*. Austin: Jenkins Publishing Co., 1973; 2nd ed.,
Norman: University of Oklahoma Press, 1996.

Berry, Mary Frances, and John W. Blassingame. *Long Memory:
The Black Experience in America*. New York: Oxford
University Press, 1982.

Brewer, J. Mason. *Aunt Dicy Tales: Snuff-Dipping Tales of the
Texas Negro*. Austin: n.p., 1956.

_____. ed. *Heralding Dawn: An Anthology of Verse*. Dallas: By
the author, 1936.

_____. *The Word on the Brazos: Negro Preacher Tales from the
Brazos Bottoms of Texas*. Austin: University of Texas
Press, 1953.

Campbell, Randolph B. *An Empire for Slavery: The Peculiar
Institution in Texas, 1821–1865*. Baton Rouge:
Louisiana State University Press, 1989.

Dailey, Maceo C. and Kristine Navarro. *Wheresoever My People
Chance to Dwell: Oral Interviews with African American Women of El Paso*. Baltimore: Black Classic Press,
1999.

Franklin, John Hope. *From Slavery to Freedom: A History of
Negro Americans*. 5th ed. New York: Alfred A. Knopf,
1980.

Giddings, Paula. *When and Where I Enter: The Impact of Black Women on Race and Sex in America*. New York: Bantam Books, 1985.

Grider, Sylvia Ann and Lou Halsell Rodenberger. *Texas Women Writers: A Tradition of Their Own* (College Station: Texas A&M University Press, 1997.)

Hall, Jacqueline Dowd. *Revolt against Chivalry: Jessie Daniel Ames and the Women's Campaign against Lynching*. New York: Columbia University Press, 1979.

Hall, Josie Briggs. *Hall's Moral and Mental Capsule for the Economic and Domestic Life of the Negro, as a Solution of the Race Problem*. Dallas: Rev. F. S. Jenkins, 1905.

Hare, Maud Cuney. *Norris Wright Cuney: A Tribune of the Black People*. New York: Crisis Publishing Co., 1913; reprint, Austin: Steck-Vaughn, 1968.

Hine, Darlene Clark, ed. *Black Women in America: An Historical Encyclopedia,* 2 vols. Brooklyn, N.Y.: Carlson Publishing Co., 1993.

Jones, Jacqueline. *Labor of Love, Labor of Sorrow: Black Women, Work and the Family, from Slavery to the Present*. New York: Vintage Books, 1986.

Lewis, David Levering. *The Portable Harlem Renaissance Reader.* Viking Penguin, April 1994.

_____. W. E. B. Du Bois: *Biography of a Race, 1868–1919*. Henry Holt & Company, Inc., September 1994.

_____. W. E. B. Du Bois: *The Fight for Equality and the American Century, 1919–1963,* Vol. 2. Henry Holt & Company, Inc. September 2000.

_____. *When Harlem Was in Vogue*. New York: Knopf: Distributed by Random House, 1981.

Malone, Ann Patton. *Women on the Texas Frontier: A Cross-Cultural Perspective.* El Paso: Texas Western Press, University of Texas at El Paso, 1983.

Mullen, Harryette. *Tree Tall Woman.* Galveston: Energy Earth Communications, 1981.

Roses, Lorraine Elena. "Harlem Renaissance." In Darlene Clark Hine, ed., *Black Women in America,* vol. 1. Brooklyn: Carlson Pub. Co., 1993. 529–32.

Roses, Lorraine Elena and Ruth Elizabeth Randolph. *Harlem Renaissance and Beyond: Literary Biographies of 100 Black Women Writers.* Boston: G. K. Hall, 1990.

Shockley, Ann Allen. *Afro-American Women Writers 1746–1933: An Anthology and Critical Guide.* New York: Meridian, 1988.

Stetson, Erlene, ed. *Black Sister: Poetry by Black American Women, 1746–1980.* Bloomington: Indiana University Press, 1981.

Werden, Frieda. "Bernice Love Wiggins." In Lina Mainiero, ed., *American Women Writers,* vol. 4. New York: Ungar Publishing Co., 1982. 414–5.

Winegarten, Ruthe. *Black Texas Women: A Sourcebook.* Austin: University of Texas Press, 1996.

———. *Black Texas Women: 150 Years of Trial and Triumph.* Austin: University of Texas Press, 1995.

Woolfolk, George Ruble. *The Free Negro in Texas, 1800–1860: A Study in Cultural Comparison.* Ann Arbor, Mich.: Published for *Journal of Mexican-American History* by University Microfilms International, 1976.

Maceo C. Dailey Jr. is the director of the African-American Studies Program of the University of Texas at El Paso and a governor's appointee to the Texas Council for the Humanities and Juneteenth Commission.

Ruthe Winegarten is a faculty associate with the Center for the Study of Women and Gender at the University of Texas in San Antonio. She has written twelve books about Texas women and Texas history, including the award-winning books *Texas Women, A Pictorial History: From Indians to Astronauts* and *Black Texas Women: 150 Years of Trial and Triumph*.